Innovation in Teaching of Research Methodology Excellence Awards 2023

An Anthology of Case Histories

Edited by Dan Remenyi

Innovation in the Teaching of Research Methodology Excellence Awards 2023: An Anthology of Case Histories

First published June 2023

Note to readers: Some papers have been written by authors who use the American form of spelling and some use the British. These two different approaches have been left unchanged.

ISBN: 978-1-914587-76-4 (PDF)

ISBN: 978-1-914587-78-8 (Printed book)

Published by: Academic Conferences International Limited, Reading, RG4 9AY, United Kingdom, info@academic-conferences.org

Available from www.academic-bookshop.com

Table of Contents

Acknowledgements

We would like to thank the judges, who initially read the abstracts of the case histories submitted to the competition and discussed these to select those to be submitted as full case histories. They subsequently evaluated the entries and made further selections to produce the finalists who are represented in this book.

Judging Team

Dr Martin Rich is Senior Lecturer in Information Management and Course Director for the BSc in Business Studies at Cass Business School. He has over twenty years of experience in building innovative approaches to teaching and learning into an established business school. Some of this centres around the possibilities opened by technological innovation and changes in the tools and online resources available to students to support their studies. He is also interested in how management education should evolve to meet the requirements of a changing business environment, and how students can best learn the skills and analytical techniques that will prepare them for a future that cannot be predicted. Martin's approach to learning places a strong emphasis on developing students' abilities as independent researchers, and on building ties between research methods and the abilities that business and management graduates can be expected to demonstrate during their careers. He is a regular participant in the ECRM track on teaching research methods and has published and presented around the subject.

Professor Anthony Mitchell PhD, DIC, MSc, BSc, CEng, FIET, FHEA is Professor of Operations Management at Ashridge Executive Education, Hult International Business School and a visiting fellow at Southampton University Business School. Following an early career in industry and consulting he spent 27 years at Ashridge Business School as a senior member of faculty including MBA director and director of postgraduate projects. Anthony has held visiting roles at Monash, Otago, EIPM, RSM and Strathclyde Business school and now has an adjunct role at Ashridge. He has taught and published in the fields of operations, continuous improvement, supply chain, strategic management and eLearning. His research interests include multinational organisations, globalisation, the role of outsourcing and offshoring, and mixed methods research methodologies.

Introduction

The Innovation in the Teaching of Research Methods Excellence Awards is an established annual event.

We continue to be encouraged by the interest which has been shown in these Excellence Awards, as we believe that the case histories recorded here are a valuable asset to those who are trying to improve their teaching of research methodology in the social sciences.

Initially 7 submissions were received, and 5 contenders were invited to submit a full case history describing their initiative. These case histories were double-blind peer reviewed, and this publication contains the entries of the shortlisted contestants. We are once again pleased to see the global reach these Awards have with contributions this year from India, Portugal, and the United Kingdom.

We feel that these case histories provide helpful insights into the types of issues academics are coping with when teaching research methodology today in various parts of the world.

Dan Remenyi
Editor
August 2023
dan.remenyi@academic-publishing.org

Using Understanding by Design and Differentiated Instruction to teach Strategy and Research Methods in Business Studies

Manuel Au-Yong-Oliveira[1] and Andrea Mangiatordi[2]
[1]INESC TEC, GOVCOPP, DEGEIT, University of Aveiro, Portugal.
[2]"R. Massa" Department of Human Sciences and Education, University of Milano-Bicocca, Italy.
mao@ua.pt
andrea.mangiatordi@unimib.it

Abstract: The idea for teaching strategy last semester according to a different methodology came from an Erasmus+ project led by the University of Milano-Bicocca and the Department of Human Sciences and Education in particular [project coordinator Andrea Mangiatordi]. The teaching described herein took place at the University of Aveiro. Teaching strategy at the master's level is a challenge, in this case involving teaching research methods, also so as to publish the students' work in research journals and international conferences. Understanding by Design (UbD) and Differentiated Instruction (DI) were used. UbD involves thinking backwards and about what we want the students to learn during the semester. This means going from defining learning objectives to developing learning materials and classroom presentations. Big ideas are defined for each lecture, as UbD states should be done, so that students may grasp the essence of what is being taught. This involved being able to define a research question, theme, and research design worth working on applied to the strategy realm. Evaluation objectives will go as far as to assess the learning regarding the anonymous peer review process and is all about making a contribution to academia - theory - and industry - practice. Some basics in SPSS statistics (chi-square test, correlations, among others) were taught and were well-received. Assignment feedback is given halfway through the semester. Of note is that this will be the first academic paper that most students will be producing, hence specific challenges exist in so far as referencing and supporting their work is concerned. As DI theory suggests, it is important to vary content, learning processes, products and learning environments. Difference goes beyond language and involves also cultural exchanges and varying perspectives of hierarchy within groups. The assignments were group efforts, and these are not always absent of conflict, which the lecturer needs to resolve (to the satisfaction of the group or at least of the most hardworking).

Related website to be visited: http://designingeducation.eu/courses/understanding-by-design-and-differentiated-instruction-for-inclusive-classrooms/

Keywords: Understanding by design, differentiated instruction, research methods, inclusive design, teaching, learning, education.

1. Introduction to the specific objectives of the teaching initiative

As a part of an Erasmus+ European funded Project entitled "InDO - Understanding by Design and Differentiated Instruction" we created a compendium of 42 innovative pedagogies with descriptions for each item, a result which was a major deliverable of the project. Having learned so much in the process and having documented the innovative pedagogies the lead author regularly used in class, as well as some others identified in the literature, the lead author proceeded to put the methodology into practice, on a Master's in Management degree course on Strategy and Competitiveness, in the academic year of 2022-2023.

The lead author must say that he fell in love with the Understanding by Design framework. It is about designing backwards what and how we want to teach. "Understanding by Design focuses on what we teach and what assessment evidence we need to collect... [it] is predominantly (although not solely) a curriculum design model" (Tomlinson and McTighe, 2006, p.2). Let us maintain quite present that: "The primary goal of quality curriculum design is to develop and deepen student understanding" (Tomlinson and McTighe, 2006, p.4).

Understanding by Design involves various steps or stages. Step 1 in backward design is to "identify desired results... as a focal point for teaching all students. The "big ideas" that we want students to come to understand" (Tomlinson and McTighe, 2006, p.33). In relation to the Strategy and Competitiveness course, these "big ideas" were determined as being, per lecture (for a total of fourteen lectures for the Winter semester):

1. The basic fundamentals of research methodology. Quantitative and qualitative research. The Scopus database. Literature reviews. Launching of group work 1 (free topic on strategy). **BIG IDEA: What remains to be studied about strategy? How can I advance the literature and make a contribution?**
2. What is strategy (Porter, 1996)? Strategic management and its future as a profession. **BIG IDEA: The strategist as a career.**
3. Strategy tools (Evans, 2014). Core competences, SMART objectives, Balanced Scorecard, Core ideology, BCG matrix, Porter's Five Forces, Opportunity cost, Porter's generic strategies, Mintzberg on emergent and deliberate strategy. **BIG IDEA: Have a complete toolkit - checklist style, advises strategist Charlie Munger. Master various strategy theories and tools.**
4. Strategy theories (Malacina and Teplov, 2022). On: Ambidexterity, Agency, Dynamic capability, Contingency, Absorptive capacity, Relational, Resource-

based, Industrial organization, Knowledge-based, Transaction cost. **BIG IDEA: Master multiple mental models that underlie reality, advises Charlie Munger.**

5. The Sage case (Oliveira et al., 2007). Growth strategies. Internationalization. Innovation. Acquisitions. Group work 1 - pitches. **BIG IDEA: Organic growth (slower, riskier) versus growth by acquisition (faster, more expensive).**
6. National cultures and the characteristics of countries. Relationship cultures. The case of Portugal (Hofstede, 2001; Solomon and Schell, 2009). **BIG IDEA: Different cultures (e.g., transaction vs. relationship) require different methods of operation.**
7. Steps towards the anchoring of change. Transformational leadership (Kotter, 1995). Kaizen (Coimbra, 2016). **BIG IDEA: Aversion to change and the lazy human being.**
8. Sustainability and strategy. Launching of group work 2 (on sustainability). **BIG IDEA: Sustainability is a current buzz word and firms cannot turn their backs on this theme.**
9. Blue ocean and red ocean strategies (Kim and Mauborgne, 2005). Low-cost firms and differentiated firms. **BIG IDEA: The emphasis on creating new business markets (blue ocean strategy) rather than entering overcrowded markets (red ocean strategy). The roles of price and of value.**
10. Mergers. Corporate governance. Group work 2 - pitches. **BIG IDEA: Merging different corporate cultures is extremely difficult and complex. Firms need to secure themselves against the ambitions of their managers and CEOs.**
11. CEOs of large corporations. The superstar CEO and their curse. **BIG IDEA: Hiring from within (someone who knows the firm and its culture) is oftentimes better than seeking superstar talent external to the firm.**
12. Negative organizations (Au-Yong-Oliveira, 2022). **BIG IDEA: Not all firms function according to a meritocracy. Beware of the *status quo* and of the often hidden "little powers" within firms.**
13. Outsourcing. Strategic alliances. Joint ventures. **BIG IDEA: Outsource only what is not essential and distinctive about the firm (do not give your competitive advantage to others).**
14. [Irrational] Decision making. The role of intuition. A review of the work by Tversky, Kahneman, and Thaler. **BIG IDEA: Psychology is central to strategy. Strategy is about people and about the decisions they make.**

In Step 2 of Understanding by Design "teachers are asked to "think like assessors" to determine the assessments that will provide the evidence for the identified knowledge, skills and understandings in step 1." (Tomlinson and McTighe, 2006, p.34).

For the assessment of strategy learnings and understandings the following assessment system was developed:

1. *Discrete evaluation* – two group projects [the best ones are published in conference proceedings or journals – please see Annex I for an example for the current year]
   1. An initial project according to the interests of the group regarding strategy; and
   2. A second project on sustainability as a pillar of strategy **– to be submitted to the annual GRACE (grace.pt) competition – each student participant receives a certificate of participation from GRACE – and their work will be evaluated by an independent jury, as well as by the teacher of the curricular unit – the University of Aveiro has won a prize of some sort every year in this competition for the last eight years and 2023 was no exception (please see image 1)**). The two projects are worth 40% each; and
   3. An individual test (on more theoretical concepts and on the language that is seen to be required in order to be hired as a strategy consultant or executive) is worth 20% of the final grade.

2. ***Evaluation by final exam*** – worth 100% of the final grade (on more theoretical concepts and on the language that is seen to be required in order to be hired as a strategy consultant or executive; short answer questions and narrative questions for deeper understanding and explanations of the influence of various strategy-related factors).

Therefore, when considering "the big ideas we want students to "understand", we need to concurrently consider the evidence that will show that students truly understand them... understanding is best revealed through various facets..." (Tomlinson and McTighe, 2006, p.34).; i.e., being able to "explain, interpret, apply, shift perspective, display empathy, and reflectively self-assess" (Tomlinson and McTighe, 2006, p.34).

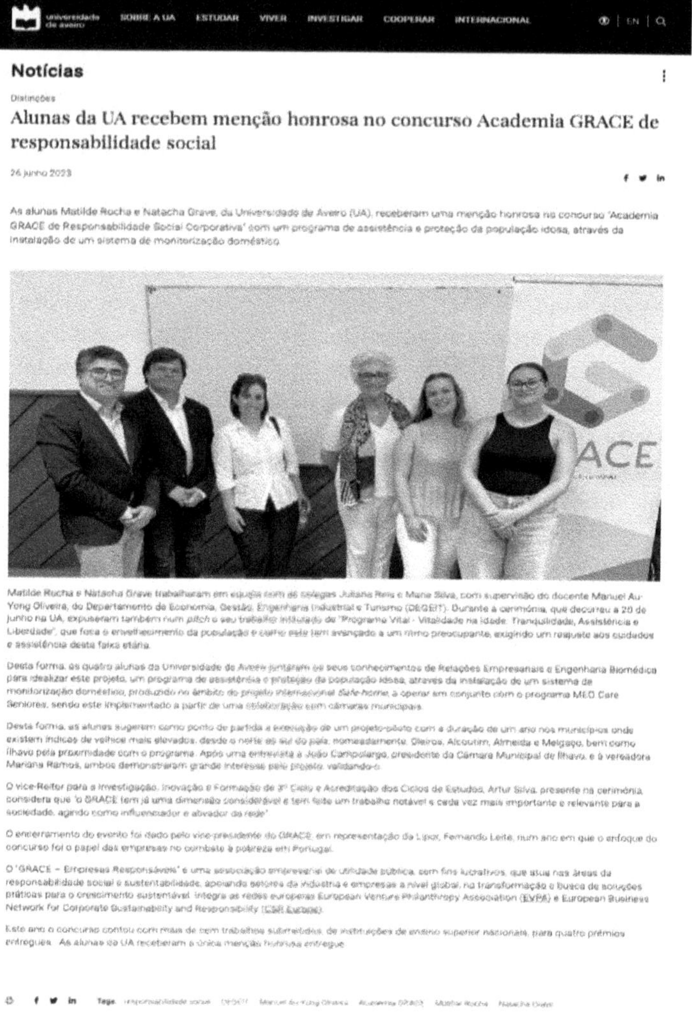

universidade de aveiro | SOBRE A UA | ESTUDAR | VIVER | INVESTIGAR | COOPERAR | INTERNACIONAL | EN

Notícias

Distinções

Alunas da UA recebem menção honrosa no concurso Academia GRACE de responsabilidade social

26 junho 2023

As alunas Matilde Rocha e Natacha Grave, da Universidade de Aveiro (UA), receberam uma menção honrosa no concurso 'Academia GRACE de Responsabilidade Social Corporativa' com um programa de assistência e proteção da população idosa, através da instalação de um sistema de monitorização doméstico.

Matilde Rocha e Natacha Grave trabalharam em equipa com as colegas Juliana Reis e Maria Silva, com supervisão do docente Manuel Au-Yong Oliveira, do Departamento de Economia, Gestão, Engenharia Industrial e Turismo (DEGEIT). Durante a cerimónia, que decorreu a 20 de junho na UA, expuseram também num *pitch* o seu trabalho intitulado de "Programa Vital - Vitalidade na Idade: Tranquilidade, Assistência e Liberdade", que foca o envelhecimento da população e como este tem avançado a um ritmo preocupante, exigindo um reajuste aos cuidados e assistência desta faixa etária.

Desta forma, as quatro alunas da Universidade de Aveiro juntaram os seus conhecimentos de Relações Empresariais e Engenharia Biomédica para idealizar este projeto, um programa de assistência e proteção da população idosa, através da instalação de um sistema de monitorização doméstico, produzido no âmbito do projeto internacional *Safe-home*, a operar em conjunto com o programa MEO Care Seniores, sendo este implementado a partir de uma colaboração com câmaras municipais.

Desta forma, as alunas sugerem como ponto de partida a execução de um projeto-piloto com a duração de um ano nos municípios onde existem índices de velhice mais elevados, desde o norte ao sul do país, nomeadamente, Oleiros, Alcoutim, Almeida e Melgaço, bem como Ílhavo pela proximidade com o programa. Após uma entrevista a João Campolargo, presidente da Câmara Municipal de Ílhavo, e à vereadora Mariana Ramos, ambos demonstraram grande interesse pelo projeto, validando-o.

O vice-Reitor para a Investigação, Inovação e Formação de 3º Ciclo e Acreditação dos Ciclos de Estudos, Artur Silva, presente na cerimónia, considera que "o GRACE tem já uma dimensão considerável e tem feito um trabalho notável e cada vez mais importante e relevante para a sociedade, agindo como influenciador e ativador da rede".

O encerramento do evento foi dado pelo vice-presidente do GRACE, em representação da Lipor, Fernando Leite, num ano em que o enfoque do concurso foi o papel das empresas no combate à pobreza em Portugal.

O 'GRACE – Empresas Responsáveis' é uma associação empresarial de utilidade pública, sem fins lucrativos, que atua nas áreas da responsabilidade social e sustentabilidade, apoiando setores da indústria e empresas a nível global, na transformação e busca de soluções práticas para o crescimento sustentável. Integra as redes europeias European Venture Philanthropy Association (EVPA) e European Business Network for Corporate Sustainability and Responsibility (CSR Europe).

Este ano o concurso contou com mais de cem trabalhos submetidos, de instituições de ensino superior nacionais, para quatro prémios entregues. As alunas da UA receberam a única menção honrosa entregue.

Tags: responsabilidade social | DEGEIT | Manuel Au-Yong Oliveira | Academia GRACE | Matilde Rocha | Natacha Grave

Image 1 – University of Aveiro news item - The lead author's University of Aveiro students Matilde Rocha, Natacha Grave, Juliana Reis, and Maria Silva had an Honourable Mention on the 20th June 2023 – at the IX GRACE Academy awards ceremony – which was held at the University of Aveiro.

Well, this can be shown through the group work/assignments. As well as through the individual test / exam. Much care will have to be taken in the forming of the test /

exam questions and in the evaluation and feedback given to the students concerning their group work. The fourteen big ideas need to be focused on and reflected in the global evaluation system.

As regards the group work the evaluation grid is as follows:

Items to be evaluated (x 10):

1. Use of academic references
2. Correct format of academic references
3. Use of recent references
4. Use of seminal papers as references
5. Formal language used
6. Contribution made to theory
7. Contribution made to practice
8. Correct use of methodological tools
9. Good story told
10. Global coherence of the study

The concept of differentiated instruction is a complex one, albeit attainable, even with a class of 135 or so students. How is this possible? How may one teach so many people, also from different countries, in a successful and satisfactory way? The issue is that amongst 135 students there will be a diverse set of learning styles – due to "culture, race, language, economics, gender, experience, motivation to achieve, disability, advanced ability, personal interests, learning preferences, and presence or absence of an adult support system are just some of the factors that students bring to school with them in almost stunning variety" (Tomlinson and McTighe, 2006, p.1).

In effect, for me there is no alternative to trying to differentiate my instruction. "Few teachers find their work effective or satisfying when they simply "serve up" a curriculum – even an elegant one – to their students with no regard for their varied learning needs" (Tomlinson and McTighe, 2006, p.1). I could not be more in agreement. For the purpose of teaching strategy and competitiveness at the master's level I resort to a number of strategies, in order to cater to the diverse learning styles and cultures in class, namely:

- Flexible grouping
- Interest-based instruction
- Responsive environment
- Plus, a powerful curriculum...

Step 3 of Understanding by Design involves the teaching and learning plan – the strategies (35 in total, in this case) used to promote understanding amongst the students in class. The objective is to cater to the diverse learning modalities of our students.

Methods / Techniques used to promote understanding in class (35 techniques listed below, the most used of the initial 42 pedagogies identified and mentioned above):

1. [Short] educational videos being shown in class to encourage the discussion of a topic
2. Read articles at home to then discuss in class
3. Slides being projected in class (traditional, more passive knowledge transfer)
4. Sharing autoethnographical experiences in class and in coursework
5. Academic research methodology being taught in class (for writing academic studies and reports)
6. Writing an academic article as an assignment - with positive criticism feedback
7. Creating exam questions in class
8. Theory being discussed in class (e.g., mental models, strategy tools and theory)
9. Practical life in organizations being discussed (storytelling)
10. Writing / creating new theory (contribution to the academic literature)
11. Group assignment - with positive criticism feedback
12. Participate in an external competition with your work / assignment - with positive criticism feedback
13. Taking notes from the whiteboard (good exercise - better than photocopies)
14. Videos / documentaries as homework
15. Publishing your work / assignment (elevating work to that next level following reviewer feedback) - with positive criticism feedback and guidance along the process
16. Doing presentations in class / a pitch, e.g., exercising communication skills
17. Doing field research (interviews, surveys, focus groups) for an assignment
18. Written individual exam - "The assessments... Thought through prior to the lessons being fully developed... define... what we want students to understand and be able to do" (Wiggins and McTighe, 2005)
19. Invited external expert speakers on specific topics
20. Online lectures (for the clarification of queries mostly linked to the group work)
21. Face-to-face physical lectures
22. Solving exercises in class quantitatively (using statistics, among others) to prove a theory
23. Distributed leadership - Have a fair extent of trust in your students and work to give them authority

24. Shared decision-making - to serve as role models for your pupils to teach them how to use these characteristics in the workplace (e.g., management by walking around in the classroom / "production environment")
25. Online Learning Management System (e-learning platform e.g., Moodle) for learning outside the classroom
26. Quizzes - with short-answers, multiple-choice - exercises created by teachers to solve in class or at home
27. Problem-based learning - Learning is organized around a problem and where the role of the teacher is less of an instructor but more of a facilitator
28. Introducing digital tools in the classroom, e.g., Basecamp project-management tool
29. Thinking-based learning, e.g., critical thinking - "Weather: A man on a walk notices that it has suddenly become cool, thinks that it is probably going to rain, looks up and sees a dark cloud obscuring the sun, and quickens his steps (Dewey, 1910, 6-10; 1933: 9–13)." (https://plato.stanford.edu/entries/critical-thinking/)

    "Disorder: A man finds his rooms on his return to them in disorder with his belongings thrown about, thinks at first of burglary as an explanation, then thinks of mischievous children as being an alternative explanation, then looks to see whether valuables are missing, and discovers that they are (1910: 82–83; 1933: 166–168)." (https://plato.stanford.edu/entries/critical-thinking/)
30. Flipped classroom for student involvement, e.g., a debate in class after reading material beforehand at home
31. Active learning, e.g., discussions, quizzes, group work
32. Case studies being discussed in class - for a greater understanding of how to employ the tools to assist decision-makers in realistic circumstances
33. Case studies being created and written in class - for profound / applied learning
34. Understanding by design - "advocating the reverse of common practice" (Wiggins and McTighe, 2005, p.17)

    "Stages of backward design - Stage 1 - identify desired results - what should students know?; Stage 2 - Determine acceptable evidence - how will we know if students have achieved the desired results? Stage 3 - Plan learning experiences and instruction - think through the most appropriate instructional activities." (Wiggins and McTighe, 2005, pp.17-18). To make student understanding (and desired results generally) more likely (Wiggins and McTighe, 2005, p.7). "The content of curriculum - its priorities should center on the big ideas and important performance tasks of the chosen topic" (Wiggins and McTighe, 2005, p.7)

35. Differentiated Instruction - flexible grouping, interest-based instruction, responsive environments... Plus a powerful curriculum. (Tomlinson and McTighe, 2006).

2. How the initiative was received by the learners / The learning outcomes that were achieved and how they were measured and evaluated

The following excerpts (figures 1 and 2) are from the Quality Guarantee System of the University of Aveiro. Translated to English by deepl.com (PRO version). 47 students answered out of a universe of 133 students (figure 1). As you can see, the TTG main result is 7.98 (figure 2) out of a maximum of 9 points, which is seen to be very satisfactory (the scale is 1 to 9).

student survey
report on a course unit
and a teacher

1st Semester | 2022-23

unid	ucuunitUnivResp n° resp % resp	
degeit	47576ESTRATEGY AND COMPETITIVENESS	14847 31.76%

teacher

unid	uu	name of lecturer	edoc no.	resp no.	% resp
degeit	mao@ua.pt	MANUEL LUÍS AU-YONG OLIVEIRA	133	47	35.34%

caption
UnivResp - universe of students responding to the pedagogical survey n°
edoc - number of students associated to the teacher in the classes
n° resp - number of students who answered the survey
% resp - percentage of responses

Figure 1 – Summary of the unit and teacher under analysis

characterization of the teacher

tab.1

perg	n1	n2	n3	n4	n5	n6	n7	n8	n9	so/na	total	valid	md	average	Sx
P18	2	1	2	0	6	2	4	8	22	0	47	47	8	7.28	2.32
P19	2	0	1	0	0	3	7	10	24	0	47	47	9	7.83	1.89
P20	1	0	0	1	0	3	6	11	23	2	47	45	9	8.00	1.55
P21	2	0	0	0	1	4	10	10	20	0	47	47	8	7.68	1.79
P22	1	0	0	0	2	0	2	6	33	3	47	44	9	8.41	1.48
P23	3	1	1	1	1	5	7	8	18	2	47	45	8	7.16	2.36
P24	1	0	0	1	0	0	1	4	39	1	47	46	9	8.59	1.41
P25	2	0	0	0	0	1	2	6	36	0	47	47	9	8.38	1.70
P26	1	1	0	0	4	3	5	10	22	1	47	46	8	7.70	1.86
P27	2	0	0	0	0	1	6	7	30	1	47	46	9	8.17	1.74
P28	1	0	0	0	1	0	1	4	39	1	47	46	9	8.61	1.34
TTG	18	3	4	3	15	22	51	84	306	11	517	506	9	7.98	1.84
P29	2	0	1	0	1	1	7	17	18	0	47	47	8	7.72	1.85

caption

P18Capacity to stimulate and motivate students for the curricular unit

P19Creation of a climate favourable to learning and to the active participation of the students

P20Stimulating students' autonomy

P21Supervision of the student's work

P22Dominion of the programmatic contents

P23Organisation of contents and activities during contact hours

P24Teaching staff punctuality

P25Availability to students P26Clarity of presentation

P27The relationship of the teacher with the student

P28Compliance with assessment rules agreed with students

TTGGroup Totals (P18-P28)

P29Overall evaluation of teacher performance

n1..n9 No. of Answers in option 1 ... No. of Answers in option 9 (scale of 1 to 9)
so/na No Opinion/Not Applicable
valid No. of valid answers (without "so/na")
md Sx Median - 50th percentile
Standard Deviation (measure of dispersion of values around their mean)

Figure 2 – Classification of the unit and teacher by the students at the end of the semester

3. Plans to further develop the initiative

We aim now to apply the same concepts to other subjects, both at the undergraduate and postgraduate levels. Subjects such as Marketing Management and the

Management of Innovation and Technology. Identifying big ideas, for example, to be communicated, may be very beneficial to all parties involved.

As the InDO Project proposal states:

"The world is changing fast and it is vital that education keeps pace. Yet, at a time when innovation is most needed, the world of education is lagging: only 38% of recent entrants to the education sector believe their school/college is adept at adopting innovations, new knowledge or methods (OECD, 2016). InDO will support educators to rise to the challenge, helping them transform their teaching methods and bring learning to life through innovative and inclusive learning spaces."

We might, on a positive note, say that this is only the beginning. A small revolution in education is in the making. With a renewed focus on educating for both hard skills (SPSS, VOSviewer, rigorous research using Scopus, among others) and soft skills (communication, working in a group, among others) we see a greater possibility of a scientific contribution being made to academia.

Acknowledgements

This work was funded by the Erasmus+ European funded Project entitled "InDO - Understanding by Design and Differentiated Instruction".

References

Au-Yong-Oliveira, M. (2022). *Negative organisations and how to overcome them. Fighting to promote innovation and change.* Faro, Sílabas & Desafios. 174 páginas. ISBN: 978-989-8842-74-9.

Coimbra, E.A. (2016). *Kaizen – Uma estratégia de melhoria, crescimento e rentabilidade. Baseado no caso real da Sakthi Portugal.* Kaizen Institute. McGraw-Hill, Madrid, Espanha.

Evans, V. (2014). *25 need to know strategy tools.* FT Financial Times Publishing.

Hofstede, G. (2001). *Culture's Consequences: Comparing Values, Behaviours, Institutions, and Organizations Across Nations.* 2nd ed. Sage Publications, New York, NY, USA.

Kim, W.C., Mauborgne, R. (2005). *Blue Ocean Strategy – How to create uncontested market space and make the competition irrelevant.* Harvard Business Review Press, Boston, MA, USA.

Kotter, J.P. (1995). Leading Change: Why Transformation Efforts Fail. *Harvard Business Review*, May-June.

Malacina, I., Teplov, R. (2022). Supply chain innovation research: A bibliometric network analysis and literature review. *International Journal of Production Economics, 251,* 108540, 1- 15.

OECD (2016). *Innovating Education and Educating for Innovation.*

Oliveira, M.A., Barandas, H., Barros, A. (2007). What do innovators do to succeed? A case study of Sage plc. *Paper* apresentado oralmente por Manuel A. Oliveira na 14th International Product Development Management Conference, EIASM – The European Institute for Advanced Studies in Management - Faculdade de Engenharia, Universidade do Porto (FEUP, UP) - 10-12 junho, 2007. *Full paper* publicado nas *proceedings* da conferência, parte 2 de 3, pp.1007-1018.

Porter, M.E. (1996). What is strategy? November-December, *Harvard Business Review.*

Solomon, C.M., Schell, M.S. (2009). *Managing Across Cultures - The Seven Keys to Doing Business with a Global Mindset.* McGraw-Hill, New York, NY, USA.

Tomlinson, C.A., McTighe, J. (2006). *Integrating Differentiated Instruction + Understanding by Design (Integrando Instrução Diferenciada + Compreensão por Design)*. Association for Supervision and Curriculum Development, Virgínia, EUA.

Wiggins, G., McTighe, J. (2005). *Understanding by design*. 2nd edition. ASCD, USA.

Annex I

One group work assignment by students - for the Winter semester of 2022-2023 - was published in the international journal *Expert Systems* – a two-star Academic Journal Guide 2021 publication by Wiley

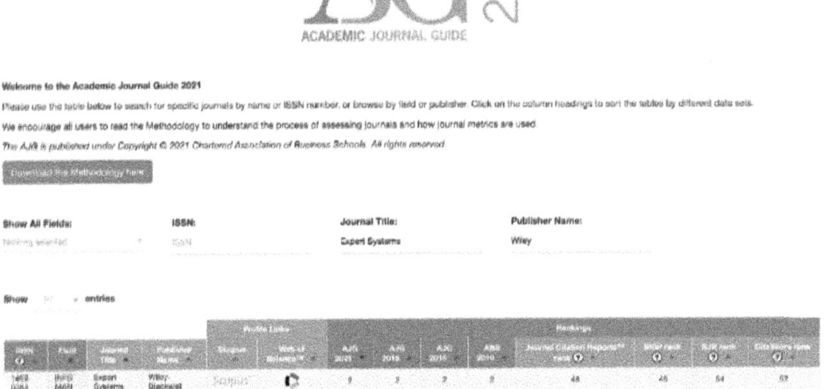

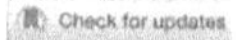

Received: 7 February 2023 | Revised: 25 May 2023 | Accepted: 3 June 2023
DOI: 10.1111/exsy.13381

ORIGINAL ARTICLE

WILEY

The impact of digital influencers on product/service purchase decision making—An exploratory case study of Portuguese people

Fábio Caiado[1] | Joana Fonseca[1] | Joana Silva[1] | Soraia Neves[1] | Ana Moreira[2,3,4] | Ramiro Gonçalves[5,6,7] | José Martins[5,7,8] | Frederico Branco[5,6] | Manuel Au-Yong-Oliveira[9]

[1]Department of Economics, Management, Industrial Engineering and Tourism, University of Aveiro, Aveiro, Portugal
[2]School of Psychology, ISPA-Instituto Universitário, Lisbon, Portugal
[3]APPsyCI—Applied Psychology Research Center Capabilities & Inclusion, ISPA—Instituto Universitário, Lisbon, Portugal
[4]Faculdade de Ciências e Tecnologia, Universidade Europeia, Lisboa, Portugal
[5]Human-Centered Computing and Information Science, INESC TEC, Porto, Portugal
[6]School of Science and Technology, University of Trás-os-Montes e Alto Douro, Vila Real, Portugal
[7]Centro de Valorização e Transferência de Tecnologia da Água, AquaValor, Chaves, Portugal
[8]EsACT-Escola Superior de Comunicação, Administração e Turismo, Instituto Politécnico de Bragança, Bragança, Portugal
[9]INESC TEC, Porto, Portugal, GOVCOPP, Department of Economics, Management, Industrial Engineering and Tourism, University of Aveiro, Aveiro, Portugal

Correspondence
Frederico Branco, Human-Centered Computing and Information Science, INESC TEC, Porto, Portugal.
Email: fbranco@utad.pt

Abstract

The growing use of technology and social media has resulted in the emergence of digital influencers, a new profession capable of changing the mentalities and behaviours of those who follow them. This study arises to better understand the potential impact digital influencers might have on the Portuguese population's purchase behaviour and patterns, and for this purpose, seven hypotheses were formulated. An online questionnaire was conducted to respond to these theoretical assumptions and collected data from 175 respondents. A total of 129 valid answers were considered. It was possible to conclude that purchase intention does not necessarily translate into a purchase action. It was also concluded that the relationship between social network use and the purchase of products/services recommended by influencers is only statistically significant for Instagram. Furthermore, the individuals' generation is not statistically significant / linked with purchasing a product/service recommended by influencers. Yet further, a small percentage of respondents have also identified themselves as impulsive shoppers and perceived Instagram as their favourite social network. With the results of this study, it is also possible to state that the influencer's opinion was classified as the last factor considered in the purchase decision process. Additionally, there is a weak negative association between purchasing a product/service recommended by influencers with sponsorship disclosure and remunerated partnership, which decreases credibility and discourages purchasing, in Portugal, a feminine culture which dislikes materialism.

KEYWORDS
consumer behaviour, digital influencers, impulsive buying, influencer marketing, information behaviour, information resources, purchase intention, social media

Author biographies

Manuel Au-Yong-Oliveira; On 1st march 2023 Manuel (PhD - FEUP, 2012; Habilitation – University of Aveiro, 2022) was awarded an honourable mention by the University of Aveiro for his research in the social sciences at the University of Aveiro Annual Researcher Awards ceremony. Manuel previously worked in industry in the management consultancy, health, book publishing, advertising, water treatment and metallurgic (gas cylinders) sectors.

Andrea Mangiatordi is a senior researcher at the University of Milan-Bicocca, Department of Human Sciences and Education. His work focuses on the application of inclusive design frameworks in teaching and learning, with a particular interest in the accessibility of digital educational content and the usability of digital platforms.

The Creation of the Novel Intuitive Feeling Research (IFR) Method

Manuel Au-Yong-Oliveira[1], Klaus Kuehnel[2] and António Gil Andrade-Campos[3]
[1]INESC TEC, GOVCOPP, DEGEIT, University of Aveiro, Portugal
[2]University of Munich, Germany; GOVCOPP, University of Aveiro, Portugal
[3]GRIDS – TEMA, Departamento de Engenharia Mecânica, Universidade de Aveiro, Portugal
mao@ua.pt
klaus.kuehnel@hotmail.com
gilac@ua.pt

Abstract: Teaching research methods and interacting with more experienced and knowledgeable Ph.D students is a challenge. Especially if they come from very developed countries (e.g., Germany). In such cases, autoethnography makes sense... because the student has so much valuable knowledge and experience to share. In one or two such cases, autoethnography, seen to be a new (or less traditional) qualitative methodology, was seen to not satisfy the requisites – regarding what was really happening in our research. Hence, we developed a new research approach – which we called Intuitive Feeling Research – or IFR. The research questions are: How should we teach research methodology to more experienced doctoral students? How may we tap and get more experienced students to share their innovative knowledge? We developed a six-step process, described herein. It is therefore a qualitative methodology based on words and narratives, coming from the "inner work environment" of the experienced individual. At a time when Bing Chat (artificial intelligence) is falling in love with humans, and when we do not know where ideas are coming from, perhaps it makes sense to tap individual unstructured knowledge from different areas in a more intuitive way? No one to date is collecting this sort of data in research, to our knowledge, from knowledgeable individuals. We need a systematic tool to collect this information. An easy way. Society will benefit. Cross-field research to improve existing company systems. The referred-to very knowledgeable students come from a new DBI program (Doctorate in Business Innovation), at the University of Aveiro. "DBI is a flexible, business context-adaptive program focused on applied results and personalized goals, dedicated to innovation and business. DBI promotes learning in a business environment, enhancing effective student skills. Students apply various methods as well as leadership skills and multidisciplinary teamwork in a doctoral level innovation project." (https://www.ua.pt/en/edua/dbi-doctorate-in-business-innovation). A lot of senior leaders are on the program with a lot of accumulated knowledge they are ready to share – via IFR? Some previous publications have tested the receptivity to the IFR method. The key methodological words in the aforementioned publications are: experience, introspection, mature writing, artificial intelligence, intuitive integration, practical observations in the field, anthropology, ethnography, and scientific approach.

Keywords: academia, industry, intuition, knowledge, research, sharing, practitioners.

1. Introduction (to the specific objectives of the initiative)

I first understood the need for a new research approach when working with experienced and very enlightened doctoral students who had a wealth of knowledge to share. How to best tap that knowledge? Would traditional research methods perform the task of knowledge transfer as well as a, perhaps, novel research gathering technique more based on intuition?

Having supervised experienced and talented students from the Doctorate in Business Innovation, at the University of Aveiro (UA), this article is an attempt at communicating what we have done in these cases - to capture and communicate new knowledge. These valuable human resources, candidates for a Ph.D degree, often possess knowledge that they want to share or "debrief" - unstructured data, via a simple process, to our knowledge non-existent at the time of writing. This is our objective, in creating the IFR method – intuitive feeling research – to fill that gap.

An essential question one might ask at the outset is: would performing additional research on this given topic add to the knowledge pool of the researcher? E.g., the performing of interviews or of a focus group. Or is the main researcher one of the most knowledgeable people in this area of research and hence would it make more sense to document / capture what they already know [beforehand, before using other research gathering techniques]?

A search on the Scopus database on 04-08-2023 with the three terms intuition AND research AND expert found 418 documents (image 1). Thus, this research has some foundation in the literature.

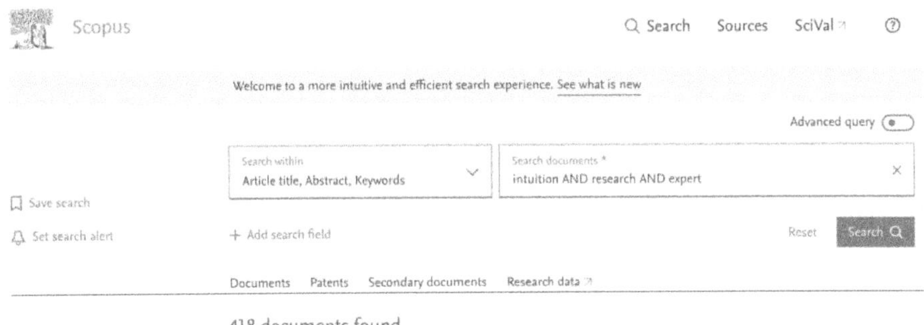

Image 1: A search on the Scopus database on 04-08-2023 with the terms intuition AND research AND expert found 418 documents

If one realizes we are talking about very knowledgeable individuals, then IFR may be a good solution to tap into that existing knowledge base. The challenge is one of "honing expert intuition" (Levy & Liguori, 2023, p.419) while considering that "human intuition remains hard to imitate" (Levy & Liguori, 2023, p.419) and that even "algorithms produce potentially biased outcomes" (Levy & Liguori, 2023, p.419).

Remember that we are not predicting the future - a task of great uncertainty and difficulty, according to Kahneman et al. (2021) for which mechanical models and formulas (e.g., statistics and multiple linear regression) beat human judgement - but more documenting the past experience of the researcher - which is an entirely different exercise. Kahneman is a great advocate of the strength of human intuition and is, in his own words, very intuitive in his decision-making. Albeit one should run the exercise of remembering the past several times before making the final decision on it as with each iteration one improves the accuracy of one's results.

2. The Doctorate in Business Innovation at the University of Aveiro

A doctoral degree is not only a very high scientific achievement and a personal milestone, but also a clever and sustainable investment in the professional future of an individual. However, the challenge of pursuing a Ph.D. is often incompatible with today's very demanding job activity. The only way to achieve a Ph.D. while at the same time working for a company is to synchronize the medium and long terms goals of both Ph.D. research and the company's developments. However, this synchronization is very hard because academia and companies seem to be living in different planets, having different time zones and chronometers. The Ph.D normally takes 3 to 4 years and must present an innovative thesis from a scientific point of view, which today is assessed by peer-review within scientific journals.

Today, companies cannot wait for four years to improve or even to update. Revenues cannot stop. The development and market adaptation must be continuous; however, breaking innovations generally take a decade.

Nevertheless, a Ph.D. can be prepared with a global vision and multi-annual planning, which aims to solve concrete problems and reinvent complex and multidisciplinary processes of companies. The goal is to achieve innovation for the company, but innovation from a scientific point of view as well. This can be done with the perfect alignment of the company with the University, and with the student as well. However, this perfect alignment is only possible if the student has the company's mindset and takes up the cudgels of the company's cause. The last decade's experience with PhDs in a non-academic environment showed that this alignment is only possible if the student comes from the company and there is a full commitment from both the student (the company's human resource) and the company.

It was in this doctoral course and environment that I came into contact with excellent and elite Ph.D students who needed to be "set free" to innovate – free from academic bonds which might hinder their career-long knowledge sharing.

3. The starting point

The UA, in its strategy of innovation and proximity to the business community, created the Doctorate in Business Innovation (DBI). However, this Ph.D. was a request from the companies, and not a product from the scientific community, as is the majority of Ph.D. degrees. Companies wanted to develop innovation inside their borders, with full ownership of the results, lower costs than service contracts and larger flexibility than the majority of funded research projects. However, multidisciplinary guidance from a non-competing institution, such as a university, was required.

It was clear that we were in a new and unique position as regards the Ph.D candidates for the DBI. They were well-above average – in terms of [career-earned] knowledge, intrinsic motivation, and the desire to learn more as well as transfer what they know to academia.

The first experience was the adaptation of the existent Ph.D. structure to the companies' requests. However, it was rapidly concluded that the classical Ph.D. curriculum, with regular 1st year classes, was not adapted to the goals of this challenge, even for the case of online classes. The curriculum phase of the DBI must be adapted to the companies' sprints (see the scrum framework). Therefore, a new structure, with "immersive" working weeks was created. In three weeks per year, the students come to the University to (i) gain the research tools and methodologies; (ii) fully dedicate their time to scientific aspects of the Ph.D; (iii) be isolated from the companies' daily problems; (iv) be immersive in a multidisciplinary innovation networking environment and (iv) meet intensively with their supervisors. These DBI immersive weeks started in the academic year of 2020/2021, with two years of pilot editions, however, with one online edition due to COVID's constraint conditions.

4. The learning outcomes which resulted in a new research method called IFR

The new methodology, developed for highly motivated and knowledgeable Ph.D students, involves a literature review (García-Peñalvo, 2022) and then autoethnographic narratives supported by the literature – based on years of experience e.g., leading international teams. The text will tend to flow intuitively in a use-case and abstraction-based process, much as Bob Dylan described he did, albeit in a separate field, the arts. Herein we also seek control over "vividness, the uncontrollable rush of a creative insight" (Lehrer, 2012) linked to perspectives in management and e.g., leadership - developed and proven in the field. These perspectives work. The communication process may be new to academia, up and beyond autoethnography – insightful narratives based on experience and discussed in view of the literature. "Imminent insight" (Lehrer, 2012) research and the need to share internal knowledge proven over time. The sole basis is past experience and a line may be being crossed in so far as giving structure to unstructured data in the brain is a challenge. Much as Amabile (1998) defends, this process attributed to "geniuses" of creativity may be much more common than we thought, and the standard human being may also be capable of abstracting and making use of information and data in the brain in this "free-flowing" fashion – writing down thoughts gathered and following a structured form. The issue is having [a great deal of] expertise to share in a given sphere or domain. The feeling is of being driven indirectly and not being controlled. This is the best feeling you can get - and is perhaps a new style of academic writing. Stay neutral and the right sequence of thought will follow – without thinking. A step beyond autoethnography and more towards "feeling" research. Unplanned. Intuitive feeling research (IFR) based on a dream – intangible thought processes. "Longing from afar". Traditional primary data collection (e.g., via interviews or focus groups) was deemed unnecessary and perhaps in certain cases this may be accepted. In the age of artificial intelligence (A.I.), where A.I. may fall in love (Roose, 2023), and we are still uncertain where these feelings come from, new avenues in research are required. The steps of IFR are seen to be:

1. Acquire expertise in a subject matter (e.g., over twenty, thirty or even forty years).
2. Find an unanswered research question following a literature review.
3. Sit in a quiet room or atmosphere (e.g., office setting) where one may focus on the topic.
4. Summon thoughts and feelings cemented over the years about e.g., a production process environment or about leadership – regarding the research question. Write them down.
5. Compare to fact-based knowledge from a database (e.g., Oracle, Scopus) to encourage the documentation process.
6. Let the feelings flow and continue to write them down in an iterative process. Challenge your intuitive conclusions several times before making them definitive.

It is therefore a qualitative methodology based on words and narratives, coming from the "inner work environment" (Amabile, 1998). The "inner work environment" is that place within ourselves where we feel content to work; where we feel good or bad about our job. The subjective element may be kept to a minimum as an objective, factual approach is adopted, confirmed by data collected over the years and by the possible participation of colleagues in the study.

Leadership is complex and multi-faceted and the text seeks to portray a wholeness of this concept. As Kahneman and Tversky (1979) stated, humans are not rational and hence when leading one needs to have present a lot of abstractions which may help us lead in practice. IFR is a result of unstructured data which exists in the mind (untapped intellectual capital) and is given a structure in the narrative form. We hope to contribute in whatever small way to a greater understanding of the complexity of research on diverse topics such as leadership.

5. A practical example of IFR

An example of IFR research follows [intuitively tapping into an expert / experienced individual's existing knowledge base]:

5.1 Leadership in Transition Research – Experience-related structure on leadership according to the understanding of the authors - A staircase for the transition in leadership

Figure 1 represents a staircase for the transition in leadership. The lower part of the figure allows the reader to add their own perspective on leadership, as each case will be different. For example, some may be more behavioural and emotional over time, without losing sight of objectivity. Leadership is a complex topic that is changing a lot in the digital world and with the increasing digitalisation of society and work.

Leadership in the modern, authentic, valuable, digital and all-encompassing environment requires a unique set of skills and attributes. Leaders must be able to think strategically, be agile and adaptable, and have a strong vision for the future. They must be able to motivate and inspire their teams, but also manage and delegate tasks effectively. They need to be able to communicate effectively and understand the importance of digital and social media in today's world. They must also be able to build relationships and foster collaboration. Finally, they must be able to create an environment of trust and respect, while also being able to make difficult decisions. In short, modern, authentic, valuable, digital and holistic leadership requires a leader who is both visionary and practical, and able to lead their team to success.

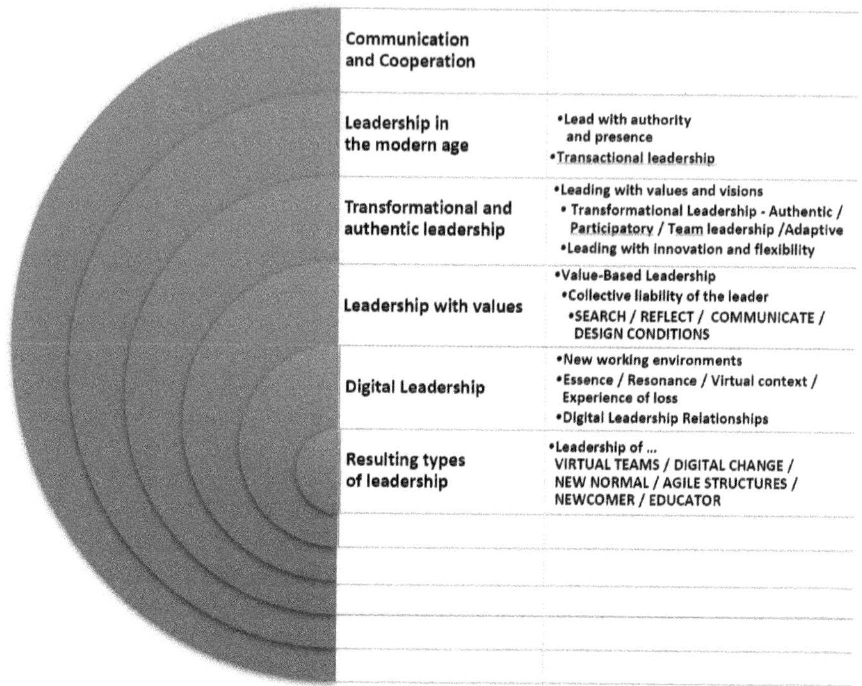

Figure 1: Staircase of the change of leadership (authors' own elaboration)

5.2 A novel look at Leadership in the face of new and old challenges

Leadership in a social and political context was already recognised and practised in antiquity (Radzilowski et al., 1994). A few centuries later, poets such as William Shakespeare or political writers such as Niccolò Machiavelli focused on the ambitions of individuals by creating portraits and stories about great leaders. The industrial age produced rational, normative and biological perspectives on leadership through the works of Karl Marx, Charles Darwin and Max Weber. Sigmund Freud and Burrhus Skinner had a stronger interest in the individual (Ives & Walsh, 2021). Psychology has shaped the modern view of leadership by, among other things, focusing on the behaviour and personality of the leader. The aspects that particularly affected a society in a particular era were therefore often reflected and related in the view of leadership (Righter & Summers, 2021). This trend can still be observed today. Diverse processes of change in social life and the so-called megatrends (table 1) mean that today's world is characterised by a great dynamism and fast pace, which has also increasingly changed the framework conditions of the world of work in recent decades. For management theory, this means that these changes are also reflected in changed management styles and that the megatrends also influence the world of management (Rollan & Somerton, 2021). One may ask the following questions:

- How do the social megatrends affect the corporate world?
- What are the consequences of social change for workers? and
- How can leaders best respond to these challenges?

Table 1: The societal megatrends (Dieguez et al., 2021)

Demographic data	- low birth rate - increasing life expectancy - Shortage of qualified workers - longer service life ... require a life-cycle oriented personnel policy (Wells et al., 2021)
Globalisation	- Increasing interconnectedness of markets and societies across national borders - global market pressure ... demands more flexibility and innovation from companies (Farini & Scollan, 2021)
Individualisation	- people's wishes and goals are more pronounced and differentiated than before - people strive for more self-determination in their life planning ... requires more flexible employment relationships and other demands on work (Miles et al., 2015)
Structural change and mechanisation	- The service sector is gaining in importance compared to the agricultural and industrial sectors. - made possible not least by the many technical achievements of modern society. ... requires more service sector jobs and a greater focus on human capital (Wilson et al., 2022)

5.3 Structure of Leadership and management styles

Leadership - a phenomenon that was just as present in ancient times as it is today. If you look at the world of work and the modern labour market, you see a society that is apparently changing faster than ever. But how can leadership be shaped today - and how can leadership styles of the future follow this change (Turpin et al., 2021)? Figure 2 describes the leadership and management styles that are considered relevant today. There is a difference between leadership and management. Leadership requires people – management, in today's technological world - does not (colleagues may be artificial intelligence or other machines). Each type of leadership may be described in-depth.

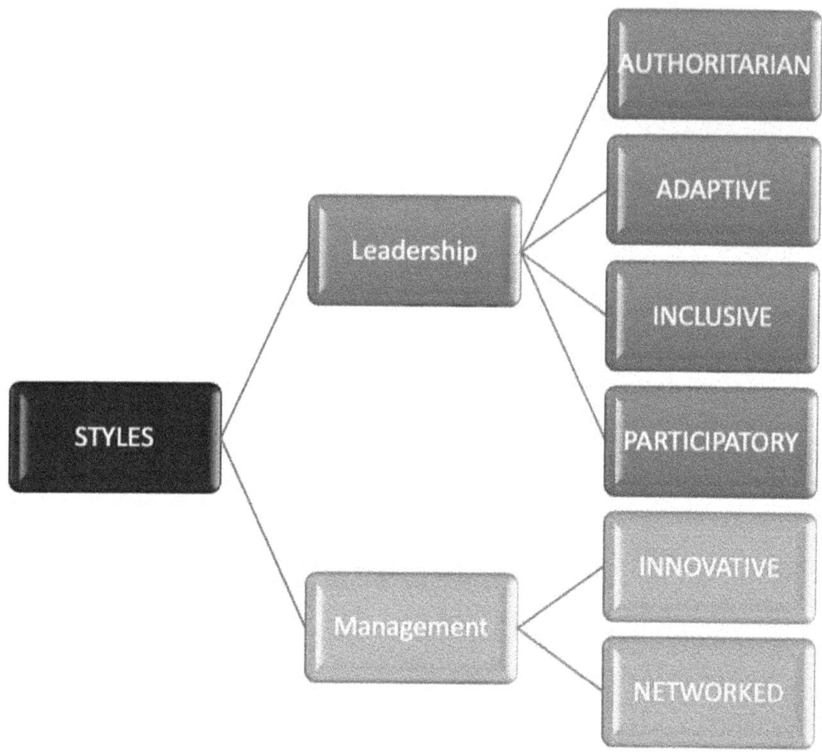

Figure 2: Leadership and management styles (authors' own elaboration)

6. IFR results and support in the literature – recent publications by the authors using IFR

Two of the coauthors of this article have published before using earlier forms of IFR. The three references in question are:

1. Kühnel and Au-Yong-Oliveira (2022) - "An artificial intelligence (AI)-based methodical analysis and synthesis approach is followed" (Kühnel & Au-Yong-Oliveira, 2022, p.609); and "clear structuring of the fields of influence, taking into account the reduction to the necessary limit possible with a system of intuitive integration of a later user; practical observations in two large corporations and various medium-sized and small companies as well as targeted data collection paired with a scientific research methodology should give the work a structural framework and guarantee success." (Kühnel & Au-Yong-Oliveira, 2022, p.615).

2. Kuehnel and Au-Yong-Oliveira (2022) – where one stated that the research was "based on observation in the field: "Seeing, hearing or sensing data relevant to the research. An observation is the identification of an occurrence of the subject being researched." (Kuehnel & Au-Yong-Oliveira, 2022, p.5, citing Remenyi, 2017, p.149). An earlier approach was also followed herein, "namely that of early anthropology, which "treated those among whom they lived and conducted their fieldwork as subjects and approached their ethnography in a detached way, believing that they were using a scientific approach, reminiscent of a positivism"" (Kuehnel & Au-Yong-Oliveira, 2022, p.5, citing Saunders et al., 2009, p.2019).
3. Au-Yong-Oliveira et al. (2023) - "This study also employs IFR - Intuitive Feeling Research – a new methodology based on researcher experience. Looking towards one's long and rich career one may realise that one harbours many of the answers, objectively, without having to seek knowledge elsewhere through interviews, focus groups or surveys. The possibility of autoethnography as a research method did not fully satisfy and our new IFR method looks beyond the above, through simplification. Not much more is needed than pen and paper (or a PC in the modern era) and some introspection and mature writing – which requires time and the mental availability to look to oneself for solutions to current societal problems." (Au-Yong-Oliveira et al., 2023, p.2)

Thus, some receptivity to the IFR method (and to several forms of the approach) does exist. The key methodological words in the aforementioned publications are: experience, introspection, mature writing, artificial intelligence, intuitive integration, practical observations in the field, anthropology, ethnography, and scientific approach.

7. Plans to further develop the initiative

The IFR method is to be tested with more such Ph.D students coming from the DBI doctoral environment, as described herein. Some very experienced students have already enquired about the method and are interested to know the next steps in order to go forward with its implementation - students who have a wealth of knowledge accumulated over an entire career, before turning to academia. Insights are also to be exchanged with the doctoral school director, one of the co-authors of this article, on the subject, and according to his accumulated experience. What may this research method signify? Is this, or a similar path, a solution to bringing some structure to an area we are only beginning to understand in the era of artificial intelligence?

Additional research is needed to test the outcomes of IFR. Further publications will work in this direction. An essential aspect for the near future is an IFR workshop to be held during an immersive week for DBI students later this year (late 2023) – which will surely test and evaluate this novel research path.

Acknowledgements

This work was partly financially supported by the Research Unit on Governance, Competitiveness and Public Policies (UIDB/04058/2020) + (UIDP/04058/2020), funded by national funds through FCT—Fundação para a Ciência e a Tecnologia; and partly financially supported by the Honourable Mention prize for the Social Sciences – University of Aveiro Researcher Awards for 2022.

References

Amabile, T.M., How to kill creativity. Harvard Business Review. September-October, 77-87, 1998.

Au-Yong-Oliveira, M., Kuehnel, K., Coutinho, E. An exploratory discussion on motivation, innovation and success in the new digital world. ICIEMC 2023 Proceedings, Nº4, 2023.

Dieguez, T., P. Loureiro, and I. Ferreira. Entrepreneurship and Leadership in Higher Education to Develop the Needed 21st Century Skills. In 17th European Conference on Management, Leadership and Governance, ECMLG 2021. 2021. Academic Conferences International Limited.

Farini, F. and A.M. Scollan, A hope to trust. Educational leadership to support mature students' inclusion in higher education: an experience from Surrey, England. International Journal of Leadership in Education, 2021. 24(5): p. 717-742.

García-Peñalvo, F.J., Developing robust state-of-the-art reports: Systematic Literature Reviews. Education in the Knowledge Soceity, 23, Article e28600. 2022.

Ives, C. and P. Walsh, Perspectives of Canadian distance educators on the move to online learning. Canadian Journal of Higher Education, 2021. 51(1): p. 28-40.

Kahneman, D., Sibony, O., Sunstein, C.R. Noise – A flaw in human judgement. William Collins, London, 2021.

Kahneman, D., Tversky, A., Prospect theory: an analysis of decision under risk. Econometrica, 47(2), March 1979.

Kühnel, K., Au-Yong-Oliveira, M. Optimal Distribution of Current Resources in a Production Environment - A Sustainable and Ethical Framework for the Digital Era. In A. Rocha et al. (Eds.), WorldCIST 2022, LNNS 470, pp. 609-619. Springer Nature Switzerland, 2022.

Kuehnel, K., Au-Yong-Oliveira, M. The Development of an Information Technology Architecture for Automated, Agile and Versatile Companies with Ecological and Ethical Guidelines. Informatics, 2022, 9(37).

Lehrer, J., The neuroscience of Bob Dylan's genius. The Guardian, April 6. 2012. Available at: https://www.theguardian.com/music/2012/apr/06/neuroscience-bob-dylan-genius-creativity, accessed on 08-03-2023. Miles, A., J.E. Asbridge, and F. Caballero, Towards a person-centered medical education: challenges and imperatives (I). Educacion Medica, 2015. 16(1): p. 25-33.

Levy, M. & Liguori, E. Algorithms and venture investment decisions: better, fairer or biased? Journal of Small Business and Enterprise Development, 2023, 30(2): p. 419-422.

Remenyi, D. Dictionary of Research Concepts and Issues, 2nd ed.; ACPI: Reading, UK, 2017.

Radzilowski, J., et al., Book Reviews. Historian, 1994. 56(2): p. 355-438.

Righter, J. and J.D. Summers. Leadership and Communication Network Identification and Analysis with Dependency Structure Matrices in Senior Design Teams. In 2021 ASEE Virtual Annual Conference, ASEE 2021. 2021. American Society for Engineering Education.

Rollan, K. and M. Somerton, Inclusive education reform in Kazakhstan: civil society activism from the bottom-up. International Journal of Inclusive Education, 2021. 25(10): p. 1109-1124.
Roose, K. (2023). A Conversation With Bing's Chatbot Left Me Deeply Unsettled. International New York Times, International Herald Tribune, Feb. 18, pp.1-3.
Turpin, M., et al., Experiences of and support for the transition to practice of newly graduated occupational therapists undertaking a hospital graduate Program. Australian Occupational Therapy Journal, 2021. 68(1): p. 12-20.
Wells, M.B., B. Kerstis, and E. Andersson, Impacted family equality, self-confidence and loneliness: a cross-sectional study of first-time and multi-time fathers' satisfaction with prenatal and postnatal father groups in Sweden. Scandinavian Journal of Caring Sciences, 2021. 35(3): p. 844-852.
Wilson, C., K. Crawford, and K. Adams, Translation to practice of cultural safety education in nursing and midwifery: A realist review. Nurse Education Today, 2022. 110.

Author Biographies

Manuel Au-Yong-Oliveira; On 1st march 2023 Manuel (PhD - FEUP, 2012; Habilitation – University of Aveiro, 2022) was awarded an honourable mention by the University of Aveiro for his research in the social sciences at the University of Aveiro Annual Researcher Awards ceremony. Manuel previously worked in industry in the management consultancy, health, book publishing, advertising, water treatment and metallurgic (gas cylinders) sectors.

Klaus Kuehnel; Graduate engineer in electrical engineering. Coach in industrial implementation of process / change management in USA, Germany, China. Lecturer at University of Munich - Academic supervisor at Bachelor / Master's level. Supervisor for startups. Consultant for industrial projects – SixSigma MasterBlackBelt. Doctoral candidate in Business Innovation. Authoring a book with Springer.

António Gil Andrade-Campos; A. Gil Andrade-Campos received his PhD in Mechanical Engineering from The University of Aveiro, Portugal, in 2005. He is an Assistant Professor of Mechanical Engineering at The University of Aveiro, research collaborator at CEMMPRE (Centre for Mechanical Engineering, Materials and Processes, University of Coimbra, Portugal) and at IRDL (Institut de Recherche Dupuy de LÙme, UMR CNRS 6027, South Brittany, France). His research interest includes inverse methods, identification and determination of constitutive model parameters, optimization methods, the use of optimization methods in mechanical systems and Shape optimization in metal forming problems.

How can Students become Junior Scientists? The five year story of a Research Methodologies and Scientific Communication Course

Ana Isabel Azevedo, Jose Manuel Azevedo, Mariana Curado Malta and Agostinho Sousa Pinto
CEOS.PP, ISCAP, Polytechnic of Porto, Portugal
aazevedo@iscap.ipp.pt
Jazevedo@iscap.ipp.pt
Mariana@iscap.ipp.pt
apint@iscap.ipp.pt

Abstract: In the academic year 2018-2019, the Master on E-Business at the Business School of the Polytechnic of Porto started to deliver classes to the students. The Research Methodologies and Scientific Communication course was considered a core course in the programmeme. This course was prepared with the primary goal of guiding the students to prepare their dissertation plans, helping to improve their levels of success in completing the dissertations. A change in the traditional approach used in the institution was implemented. Firstly, the course was strategically included in the second semester of the first year of the programmeme, while traditionally, this course was included in the first semester of the second year. Secondly, the students collaborate with their potential supervisors from the beginning of the process; teachers with research interests aligned with the programmeme were invited to present their research projects to the students, pointing out future research directions, and students are allowed to choose their prefered ones or to present their own ideas for research. Thirdly, some regular workshops are organised during the semester with some invited specialists in specific areas, such as specific research methodologies and methods or software for the analysis of qualitative or quantitative data or scientific writing. Fourthly, the Summer Symposium of the Master on E-Business is organised at the end of the semester. During the symposium, the students' plan is assessed by a jury, which helps to prepare the students for their final dissertation defence. Last but not least, the students must prepare a scientific article that follows the submission and revision process of scientific conferences and journals. Easychair was used as the supporting platform in the first three years, but in the last two years, the Bulletin of the Master on E-Business was created, and the two first editions are available online. The results are promising. Data collected suggests that the success rates are better in the Master on e-business compared to the other master programmemes in the institution. Also, some students applied for research scholarships, while others are doing PhDs.

Keywords: scientific research, scientific article, starting the research, study design, scientific writing, research project

1. Case history

In the academic year 2018-2019, the Master on E-Business at the Business School of the Polytechnic of Porto started to deliver classes to the students. The programmeme was structured in four semesters. The Master's programmeme followed the traditional European standards for two years, divided into four semesters, with 120 European Credit Transfer and Accumulation System (ECTS). During the second academic year, students develop a Dissertation, a Project, or a Curriculum Internship to conclude the programmeme and get the degree (Azevedo et al., 2019).

The Research Methodologies and Scientific Communication (RMSC) course was considered a core course in the programmeme. Traditionally, in the institution, the courses on research methodologies available in the several master programmemes are provided mainly with traditional lectures. The RMSC course in the Master on E-Business represented a break with this traditional approach, introducing new dynamics in the institution. It was prepared with the primary goal of guiding the students to prepare their research plans, helping to improve their success in completing the research Dissertation, Project, or Curriculum Internship. The course provides a context for discussion and learning on the importance of study and research, developing knowledge about several qualitative and quantitative research approaches and methods to collect and analyse research data, and provides insights on developing scientific communication. In addition, the scientific board of the programmeme also intends to develop students' interest and enthusiasm in scientific research, thus having the possibility of becoming Junior scientists.

Besides the traditional lectures necessary to provide the basics of scientific research, some other strategies were used to achieve the goals defined above. A five-folded approach was used to implement changes to the traditional methods used in the institution for courses on research methodologies. Five strategies were implemented:

- Curricular placement of the course
- Collaboration with the supervisors since the very beginning
- Invited talks
- Summer Symposium
- Research Bulletin of the Master on E-Business

This approach represents a novelty in the institution where this case study was implemented since it represented a prominent shift in the traditional mindset of the institution. The new dynamics are starting to contaminate other masters in the institution, which already started connecting students with the supervisors from the beginning and organising master symposiums and scientific publications, for instance, in edited books.

2. Brief presentation of the course

Research methodologies courses are intended to provide fundamental research competencies to graduate students (Asale & Farsani, 2023; Daniel et al., 2018) as well as to undergraduate students (Gurung & Stoa, 2020). There is a vast diversity of competencies to be acquired. According to Asaie & Frasani (2023, p. 2), "these competencies can be acquiring a deep understanding of quantitative, qualitative, and mixed methods research, analysing the strengths and weaknesses of different research methods, identifying and formulating research questions, reviewing the literature, designing a research study, reporting the findings, developing critical and reflective thinking about designing, implementing, or managing research, and evaluating the quality of published studies". The course design thus involves a balance between the time available and the necessary hard and soft competencies, which was done with the RMSC course.

The RMSC course was included in the 2nd semester of the 1st year of the Master in E-Business with a workload of 3 hours per week, corresponding to 6.0 ECTS credits.

The syllabus was structured in two modules, as follows:

Module 1

1. Introduction to the scientific method
2. Primary research methodologies in IS
3. Data collection and analysis in scientific research
4. Ethical issues in scientific research

Module 2

1. The Literature Review: matrix of concepts
2. The literature search:

    4. Traditional libraries, digital libraries, closed and open access knowledge bases;
    5. Techniques and syntaxes of search in information retrieval on the WWW.

1. Bibliographic references:

    1. Standards and styles;
    2. Tools for managing citations, references and information organisation.

2. Structuring and writing scientific publications: scientific articles, book chapters, reports, posters, monographs, and thesis.

1. Organisation of information:

3. Channels of scientific communication:

   1. Scientific Journals: Submission, review and publication process.
   2. Scientific Meetings

Expository, demonstrative and active methodologies were applied based on theoretical exposition, practical demonstration and individual and group work development. It was also foreseen the use of practical cases as a methodology for acquiring analysis skills, as a way to improve the critical spirit and synthesis and communication skills.

Following the rules of the institution, it was planned to assess students according to one of the following assessment schemes:

1. Continuous assessment;
2. Final assessment.

Applying continuous assessment are considered approved in the course the students who obtain a final classification (FC) greater than or equal to 10, resulting from the application of the weighting criteria indicated in the following components of the evaluation,

Dissertation Plan/Project/Internship (PI)
Weighting Criterion: 50%

State of the Art (SA)
Weighting Criterion: 30%

Review Process (RP)
Weighting Criterion: 20%

The FC will be calculated using the following formula:

CF = PI * 50% + SA * 30% + RP * 20%

If the student does not obtain approval through the continuous assessment, he/she will be subject to the final assessment regime. The final assessment will be conducted through a "public test", carried out through a public act of presentation and defence of the work developed before an evaluation jury established for this purpose.

For the state of the art, the students conduct a systematic literature review intended to know the state of the art in the area of research they previously defined. One fundamental aspect is the identification of the research gaps in the area. This leads to the definition of the research question and of the research objectives, that is to say, the "What" of the research. After this, the students can define the adequate research methodology, and respective methods, to achieve the research objectives – the "How" of the research. These aspects are included in the research plan jointly with the ethical issues involved, a timetable, and a tentative structure for the dissertation. At the end of the semester, each student presents their plan and discusses it. They also write a scientific article of the literature review.

Due to the success of the RMSC course, the possibility was opened to include a class for Erasmus students on mobility. Thus, during its third edition (the academic year 2020/2021), the RMSC course gained a new class of international students. It was defined jointly with the teacher of the Erasmus class that the same dynamic would be implemented for this class. Nevertheless, some adjustments were necessary since the mobility students could not present the dissertation plan because they were not part of the Master on E-Business; they were mobility students attending just that course of the programme. Consequently, it was defined that the students would develop a full paper involving data collection and data analysis instead of the research plan.

Concerning the review process, it was defined that it should be implemented as close as possible to a real-life context situation. A double-blind peer review process was implemented, with the students acting as peers and the teacher acting as scientific journal editor.

Moodle's learning management system was used to support the classes in providing the necessary materials, for the students to submit the assessment elements, and for the teacher to provide additional individual feedback.

In the following sections, the five strategies used to implement changes to the traditional methods used in the institution are detailed.

2.1 Curricular placement of the course

The course was strategically included in the second semester of the first academic year of the programme, while traditionally, in the institution, this course was included in the first semester of the second academic year. The rationale behind this option was two-folded. Firstly, suppose the students start to develop the research plan in the first semester of the second academic year. In that case, it will be too late since, from the experience of the members of the scientific board of the programme, several students took too long to define the "why" of the research. Consequently, when they finally define the research approach and respective data collection and analysis methods, they do not have the time to conclude the instruments for data collection, collect, and analyse the data in due time. Secondly, including the course in the second semester of the first academic year will be too early because the students were too inexperienced and did not have contact with any of the possible topics of the programme.

Placing the course in the second semester of the first academic year was thus considered the ideal option. That way, the students have already obtained some level of maturity to decide on an adequate topic. They can define the "why" of the research early, giving them time to define the research approach and methods for data collection and analysis. Also, if, for some reason, the students found out that the topic is not appropriate for research, they still have time to redefine all the necessary.

2.2 Collaboration with the supervisors since the very beginning

The students collaborate with their potential supervisors from the beginning of the process. At the beginning of the semester, teachers with research interests aligned with the programme are invited to present their research projects to the students, pointing out future research directions. Following this presentation, students can choose the ones aligned with their interests. Also, the students can present their own ideas for research. In this case, the scientific board of the course can help the students find an adequate supervisor.

A strong connection is thus established between students and their supervisors from the beginning of the process, helping enhance it. In addition, if some incompatibility is developed, it will still be time to redefine the supervisor for the student and vice-versa, as well as the research topic, mainly considering that they start working together in the first academic year. It is worth emphasising that only in the programme's first edition did these problems occur with one student and the assigned supervisor. The problem was promptly solved, and the student could obtain the degree in due time.

2.3 Invited talks

Some regular talks were organised during the semester with some invited specialists on specific topics. The talks allowed the students to have contact with diversified scientific events and access to specialists providing them to benefit from their experience. The talks' topics differed yearly, depending on the invited specialists' availability and the student's necessities.

Three talks were provided to the students in the first edition of the course addressing the topics "Case Study in interpretivism studies", "SPSS™ for quantitative data analysis", and "Ethical issues in scientific research".

In the second edition of the course, after five weeks of classes, the lock-out defined by the Portuguese government in mid-March 2020 posed several challenges. During this first lockdown, the teacher and the students put a solid effort into adapting to online classes. Nevertheless, it was only possible to organise three talks before the lockdown took part, despite five talks being initially planned. These three talks addressed the topics "Design Science Research", "Action-Research", and "Grounded Theory".

Despite (because, I may say!) the lockdowns that took part during the third edition of the course, it was possible to organise seven talks during the semester, taking advantage of the increased facility of the lecturers to attend from their homes using Zoom™. In this edition, the talks addressed the topics "Grounded Theory", "Design Science Research", "Action- Research", "Delphi method", "Structural Modelling Equations with Amos™", "Scientific Writing", and "Ethical Issues in Scientific Research". Figure 1 presents the promotional poster for the third edition of the talks. The institution's Communication and Public Relations Office team prepared the promotional posters and disclosed the information through the organisation. The talk about scientific writing was delivered in English so the Erasmus students could attend.

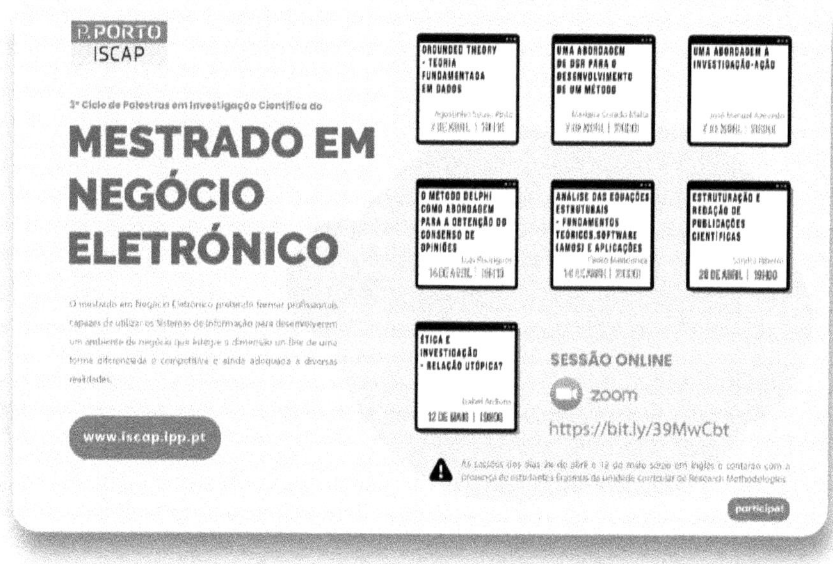

Figure 1: Promotional poster for the third edition of the talks.

NOTE: These are the original posters developed by the institution's Communication and Public Relations Office. Those materials are not available in English. The same goes for the materials presented in Figures 2 and 6.

During the fourth edition of the course, the classes returned to the face-to-face format. It was then possible to organise six talks addressing the topics "Design Science Research", "Action- Research", "Delphi method", "Structural Modelling Equations with

Amos^{TM}", "Analysing microdata using Sabi database", and "Ethical Issues in Scientific Research". Figure 2 presents the promotional poster for the fourth edition of the talks, also prepared by the institution's Communication and Public Relations Office team.

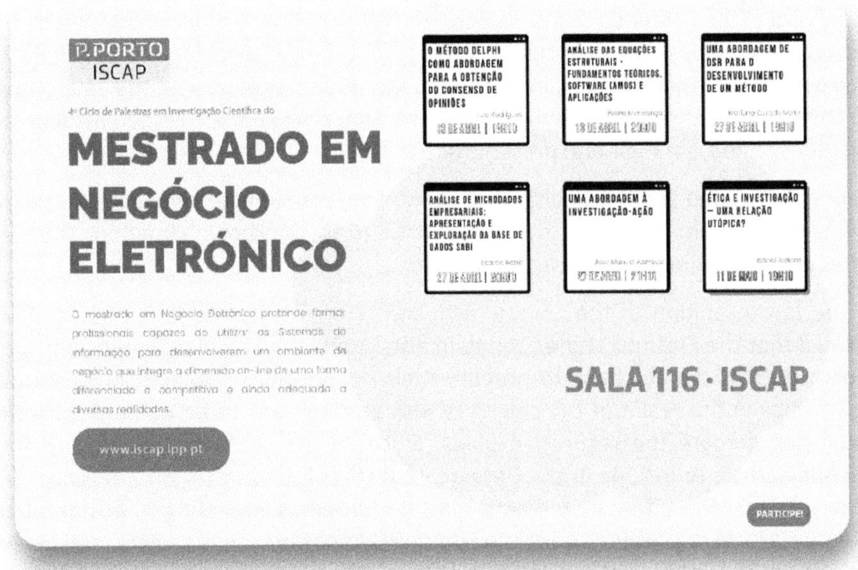

Figure 2: Promotional poster for the fourth edition of the talks.

In the fifth edition of the course, it was impossible to organise the talks due to several constraints related to the teacher's new organisational duties at the beginning of the course. Nevertheless, since for all the editions of the talks, the students found that the talks were enriching and complemented the regular classes, it is planned to implement the talks in the sixth edition.

3. Summer Symposium

The Summer Symposium of the Master on E-Business is a public event organised at the end of each semester. Each student defends the research plan before a jury during the symposium. The jury's composition is similar to the one in the final defence of the dissertation, comprising the president, the course teacher as the opponent, and the supervisor. This defence aims mainly to prepare the students for their final dissertation, project, or curriculum internship defence necessary to conclude the degree (VIVA). By participating in this event, the students get used to the environment of the final defence, learn how to present and discuss their research ideas and decisions, and train their oral presentation skills.

During the second and third editions of the course, the Summer Symposium took part online using Zoom™, such as the classes, due to the lockdown situation. The same structure was maintained for the symposium.

In the fourth edition of the course, with the return to face-to-face classes, it was defined that the Erasmus students should also attend the Summer Symposium. Since those students did not have to prepare their Dissertations, Projects, or Curriculum Internships in the realm of the course, a new strategy was to be defined since they could not prepare the respective plans. Since all the students had to prepare a scientific article to include in the Research Bulletin of the Master on E-Business (see next section), the alternative found was the students preparing a poster of the scientific article to present during the Summer Symposium. Thus a poster session was included in the programme of the symposium. The poster presentation allowed the students, both the regular and mobility students, to make contact with one more way of scientific communication. This edition's Erasmus students come from the following countries: Quirguistão (Student in Poland), Poland, Spain, France, Czech Republic, Switzerland, Latvia, Finland, Romania, Turkey, and the Netherlands.

During the fifth edition, the structure of the symposium was maintained with success since both regular and Erasmus students appreciated the connection and the sharing of experiences, similar to the previous academic year. This edition's Erasmus students come from the following countries: Ukraine, Germany, France, Poland, Latvia, Slovenia, Albania, Spain, Turkey, and Slovenia.

Figure 3 presents some selected photos of the IV Summer Symposium, the first edition that counted with the participation of international students presenting their posters.

All the news about the events are regularly published on the Facebook page of the Master on E-Business[1].

Figure 3: Some photos of the first Symposium of the Master on E-Business with international students. From left to right, from up to down: the posters of the Erasmus students, one student defending their plan before the jury, the audience of the symposium, four pictures of Erasmus students presenting their posters

4. Research Bulletin of the Master on E-Business

The RMSC course also includes the dimension of the students acquiring written scientific communication skills and making contact with a real-life submission and peer revision process. To attain that goal, the students must prepare a scientific article, submit it, participate in the peer-review process by reviewing at least two colleagues'

---

[1] https://www.facebook.com/people/Mestrado-em-Neg%C3%B3cio-Eletr%C3%B3nico-ISCAPPPORTO/100057432369822/

papers, revise their own papers, and submit the revised version, including appropriate answers to the reviewers.

Easychair was used as the supporting platform in the first two editions of the course. Figure 4 presents the list of the submissions made by the students in the Easychair platform for the first edition of the course. Only the students were considered authors of the articles during this first edition of the course.

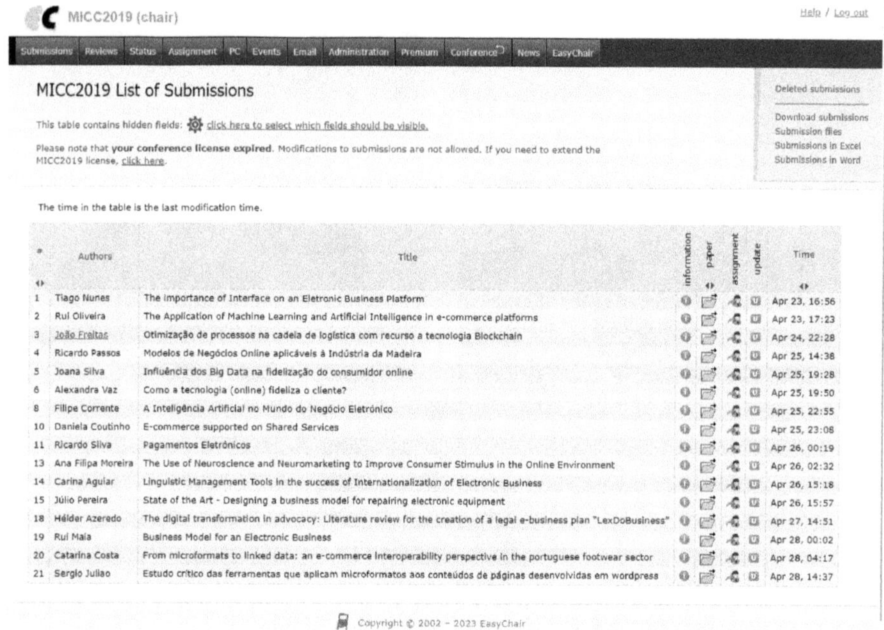

MICC2019 (chair)

Help / Log out

Submissions | Reviews | Status | Assignment | PC | Events | Email | Administration | Premium | Conference | News | EasyChair

MICC2019 List of Submissions

This table contains hidden fields: click here to select which fields should be visible.

Please note that **your conference license expired**. Modifications to submissions are not allowed. If you need to extend the MICC2019 license, click here.

Deleted submissions

Download submissions
Submission files
Submissions in Excel
Submissions in Word

The time in the table is the last modification time.

#	Authors	Title	information	paper	assignment	update	Time
1	Tiago Nunes	The importance of Interface on an Eletronic Business Platform					Apr 23, 16:56
2	Rui Oliveira	The Application of Machine Learning and Artificial Intelligence in e-commerce platforms					Apr 23, 17:23
3	João Freitas	Otimização de processos na cadeia de logística com recurso a tecnologia Blockchain					Apr 24, 22:28
4	Ricardo Passos	Modelos de Negócios Online aplicáveis à Indústria da Madeira					Apr 25, 14:38
5	Joana Silva	Influência dos Big Data na fidelização do consumidor online					Apr 25, 19:28
6	Alexandra Vaz	Como a tecnologia (online) fideliza o cliente?					Apr 25, 19:50
8	Filipe Corrente	A Inteligência Artificial no Mundo do Negócio Eletrónico					Apr 25, 22:55
10	Daniela Coutinho	E-commerce supported on Shared Services					Apr 25, 23:08
11	Ricardo Silva	Pagamentos Eletrónicos					Apr 26, 00:19
13	Ana Filipa Moreira	The Use of Neuroscience and Neuromarketing to Improve Consumer Stimulus in the Online Environment					Apr 26, 02:32
14	Carina Aguiar	Linguistic Management Tools in the success of Internationalization of Electronic Business					Apr 26, 15:18
15	Júlio Pereira	State of the Art - Designing a business model for repairing electronic equipment					Apr 26, 15:57
18	Hélder Azeredo	The digital transformation in advocacy: Literature review for the creation of a legal e-business plan "LexDoBusiness"					Apr 27, 14:51
19	Rui Maia	Business Model for an Electronic Business					Apr 28, 00:02
20	Catarina Costa	From microformats to linked data: an e-commerce interoperability perspective in the portuguese footwear sector					Apr 28, 04:17
21	Sergio Juliao	Estudo crítico das ferramentas que aplicam microformatos aos conteúdos de páginas desenvolvidas em wordpress					Apr 28, 14:37

Copyright © 2002 – 2023 EasyChair

Figure 4: Submissions on the Easychair platform for the first edition of the course

Figure 5 presents the list of the submissions made by the students in the Easychair platform for the second edition of the course. During this second edition of the course, the supervisors were also invited as authors of the articles, closer to a real-life situation.

The Easychair platform was adequate for the submission and revision process, but the need to complete the process until final publication arose. The Bulletin of the Master on E-Business was created during the third edition of the course. The first two volumes of the Bulletin of the Master on E-Business are already available online at https://www.iscap.pt/ebusiness-rj/index.php/mne-rj/index. The third volume is being prepared and is not yet available online when writing this case. Students were enthusiastic about making their scientific articles publicly available and worked hard to achieve this aim. The scientific board of the Master on E-Business prepared an editorial for the two volumes already available. The second volume includes the Editorial in Portuguese and English and also counts with the articles of the Erasmus students.

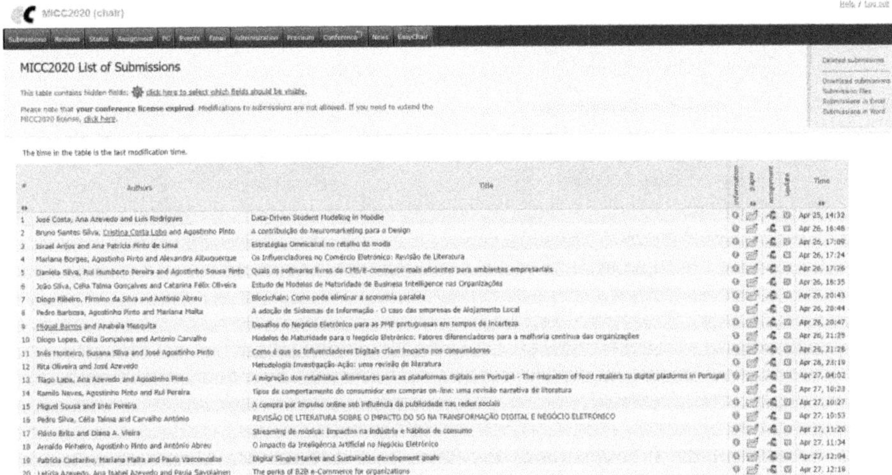

MICC2020 List of Submissions

The time in the table is the last modification time.

#	Authors	Title	Time
1	José Costa, Ana Azevedo and Luís Rodrigues	Data-Driven Student Modeling in Moodle	Apr 25, 14:32
2	Bruno Santos Silva, Cristina Costa Lobo and Agostinho Pinto	A contribuição do Neuromarketing para o Design	Apr 26, 16:48
3	Israel Anjos and Ana Patrícia Pinto de Lima	Estratégias Omnicanal no retalho da moda	Apr 26, 17:09
4	Mariana Borges, Agostinho Pinto and Alexandra Albuquerque	Os Influenciadores no Comércio Eletrónico: Revisão de Literatura	Apr 26, 17:24
5	Daniela Silva, Rui Humberto Pereira and Agostinho Sousa Pinto	Quais os softwares livres de CMS/E-commerce mais eficientes para ambientes empresariais	Apr 26, 17:26
6	João Silva, Célia Talma Gonçalves and Catarina Félix Oliveira	Estudo de Modelos de Maturidade de Business Intelligence nas Organizações	Apr 26, 18:35
7	Diogo Ribeiro, Firmino da Silva and António Abreu	Blockchain: Como pode eliminar a economia paralela	Apr 26, 20:43
8	Pedro Barbosa, Agostinho Pinto and Mariana Malta	A adoção de Sistemas de Informação - O caso das empresas de Alojamento Local	Apr 26, 20:44
9	Miguel Barros and Anabela Mesquita	Desafios do Negócio Eletrónico para as PME portuguesas em tempos de incerteza	Apr 26, 20:47
10	Diogo Lopes, Célia Gonçalves and António Carvalho	Modelos de Maturidade para o Negócio Eletrónico: Fatores diferenciadores para a melhoria contínua das organizações	Apr 26, 21:25
11	Inês Monteiro, Susana Silva and José Agostinho Pinto	Como é que os Influenciadores Digitais criam impacto nos consumidores	Apr 26, 21:28
12	Rita Oliveira and José Azevedo	Metodologia Investigação-Ação: uma revisão de literatura	Apr 26, 23:19
13	Tiago Lapa, Ana Azevedo and Agostinho Pinto	A migração dos retalhistas alimentares para as plataformas digitais em Portugal - The migration of food retailers to digital platforms in Portugal	Apr 27, 04:02
14	Ramilo Neves, Agostinho Pinto and Rui Pereira	Tipos de comportamento do consumidor em compras on-line: uma revisão narrativa de literatura	Apr 27, 10:23
15	Miguel Sousa and Inês Pereira	A compra por impulso online sob influência da publicidade nas redes sociais	Apr 27, 10:27
16	Pedro Silva, Célia Talma and Carvalho António	REVISÃO DE LITERATURA SOBRE O IMPACTO DO 5G NA TRANSFORMAÇÃO DIGITAL E NEGÓCIO ELETRÓNICO	Apr 27, 10:53
17	Fábio Brito and Diana A. Vieira	Streaming de música: Impactos na indústria e hábitos de consumo	Apr 27, 11:20
18	Arnaldo Pinheiro, Agostinho Pinto and António Abreu	O impacto da Inteligência Artificial no Negócio Eletrónico	Apr 27, 11:34
19	Patrícia Castanho, Mariana Malta and Paulo Vasconcelos	Digital Single Market and Sustainable development goals	Apr 27, 12:04
20	Letícia Azevedo, Ana Isabel Azevedo and Paula Savolainen	The perks of B2B e-Commerce for organizations	Apr 27, 12:18

Figure 5: Submissions on the Easychair platform for the second edition of the course

The Bulletin of the Master on E-Business uses the Open Journal System (OJS) software. The IT department of the school configured a server dedicated to the Bulletin and installed the software. The plugin allowing indexation on Google Scholar was activated. When writing this case, some citations are already made to some of the articles of the first two volumes of the Bulletin.

The partnership with the Research Center on the institution allowed attributing Digital Object Identifiers (DOI) to all the articles and to each of the volumes of the Bulletin. Thus the articles are part of the CrossRef directory.

The institution's Communication and Public Relations Office team prepared a Cover for the Bulletin of the Master on E-Business for both volumes available. The cover was created both in Portuguese and in English. Figure 6 presents the covers for the first volume of the Bulletin. The covers' image is coherent with the image of the promotional posters of the talks, helping to create an image for the Master on E-Business.

Figure 6: Cover for the first volume of the Research Bulletin of the Master on E-Business; Portuguese and English versions.

5. Some numbers and students' opinions

The graduates of the first edition of the Master on E-Business occur in the academic year 2019/2020.

During the first edition of the course, of the 24 students initially enrolled in the programme, 16 (66,7%) defended their proposals and succeeded in the RMSC. This first edition of the Master on E-Business got 12 of the 16 students who succeeded in the RMSC course (75%) to graduate on due time, i.e., after two academic years.

On the second edition of the course, of the 25 students initially enrolled in the programme, 20 (80%) defended their proposals and succeeded in the RMSC. This second edition of the Master on E-Business got 13 of the 20 students who succeeded in the RMSC course (65%) to graduate on due time, i.e., after two academic years. Four students took one more year to graduate. Thus, 17 in 20 students who succeeded in the RMSC course (85%) in this second edition concluded graduation.

Considering the regular students of the course's third edition, of the 25 students initially enrolled in the programme, 23 (92%) defended their proposals and succeeded in the RMSC. This third edition of the Master on E-Business got 12 of the 23 students who succeeded in the RMSC course (52%) to graduate on due time, i.e., after two academic years. Even so, some students are still working to graduate during this academic year, which is not yet finished when writing this case.

Considering the regular students of the fourth edition of the course, of the 27 students initially enrolled in the programme, 18 (66,7%) defended their proposals. The students of this fourth edition of the programme are still working to conclude their Dissertations, Projects or Curriculum Internships, so there are not yet graduates at the time of writing this case.

In the fifth edition of the course, of the 23 students initially enrolled in the programme, 16 (70%) have defended their proposals. They will work on their Dissertations, Projects or Curriculum Internships during the next academic year.

As for the Erasmus students, the success rates are excellent since only one student could not approve in the three academic years. The Erasmus students were asked to provide some feedback about their experiences. We emphasise that some Erasmus students did not have experience and liked the course; they liked being heard and interacting with other teachers invited for the talks. Also, they found out that Moodle is vital to support the classes. Some students also found a little lost along the way and suggested to "slow the pace down".

Figure 7 presents some opinions of some of the Erasmus students.

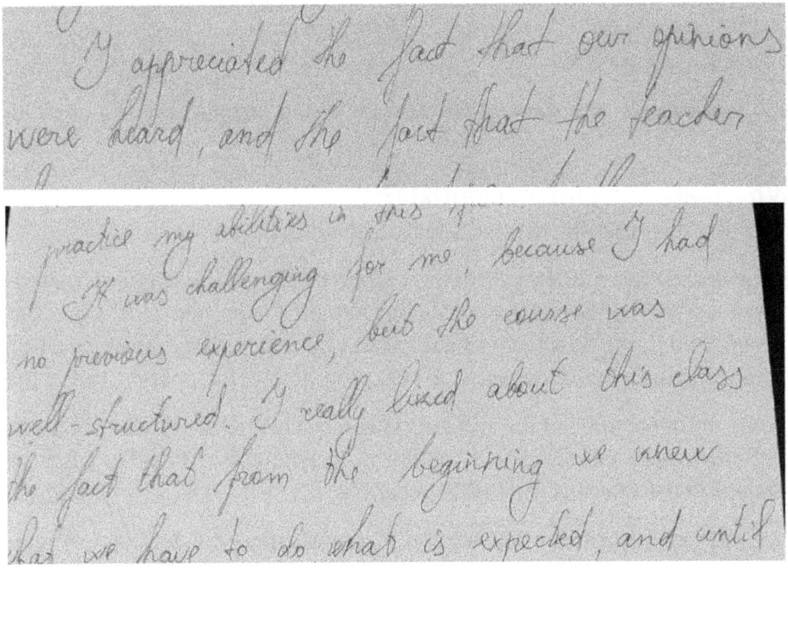

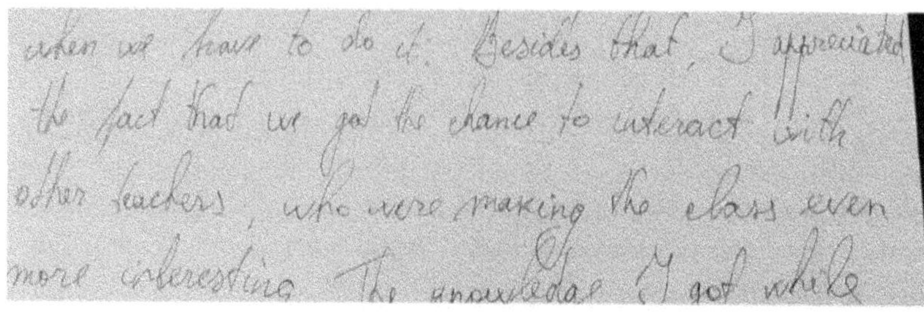
when we have to do it. Besides that, I appreciated the fact that we got the chance to interact with other teachers, who were making the class even more interesting. The knowledge I got while

For someone who usually does not enjoy writing essays or research papers, I really enjoyed this class. It was really useful that there where many files in Moodle about the research and how / what to write in it.

Thank you for the course. There was a lot of thorough information regarding the writing of scientific articles, however at points I found myself feeling a bit lost, so I ~~was~~ would have maybe slowed the pace down.

Figure 7: Five pictures with some of the opinions of the Erasmus students when asked for feedback

6. Where are the junior scientists?

When writing this case, the Master is in its fifth edition.

There are already two students from the second edition of the master enrolled in PhD programmes. This is an important achievement, even more if the context is considered. Due to the dual higher education system in Portugal, the institution being a polythetic institution, can not provide PhD programme; fortunately, this is changing.

Also, some students applied for and got research scholarships. There are already ten students from the several editions of the programme that benefits from research scholarships in the realm of the research centre.

Last but not least, since the first edition of the Master on E-Business, the students regularly publish articles in conferences, books and journals with their supervisors.

As for the other students, most of them were able to get employment in areas directly connected with the master, and some were invited to seminars and other events organised in the institution. Worth emphasising that some of the Alumni receive students of the master for internships and projects in their companies.

7. Discussion

The results of implementing the RMSC course in the Master on E-Business programme have been positive. The students have shown a high level of engagement and interest in the course, and the quality of the research plans and the scientific articles produced by the students has been high.

The lockdowns due to the COVID-19 pandemic can be considered disruptive. Due to the lockdown situation, the students did not have face-to-face meetings with their supervisors; thus, it was more challenging to establish a strong link between students and their respective supervisors, despite some efforts to conduct regular Zoom meetings. This was particularly difficult for the students of the third edition of the course (academic year 2020/2021) that started all the courses online due to the lockdown.

There were also some positive consequences of the lockdown. During the third edition of the RMSC, more students attended classes and were able to defend their proposals with success during the Summer Symposium. It was easier for the students to attend classes online since they did not have to lose time in traffic to go to school. Nevertheless, there were too few graduates in due time. We consider that an explanation is that these students could not create strong links between themselves and their respective supervisors due to the lockdowns.

The management bodies of the institution provided support to help overcome the difficulties derived from the lockdown. The Directive Board of the institution provided the necessary technological infrastructure for online classes and assessment, namely the improvement of the capabilities of the servers that hosted Moodle and institutional access to Zoom™, provided by the National Foundation for Science and Technology. They also provided the necessary regulatory directions. The Pedagogical Board organised online training sessions to prepare the teacher for online classes.

In the future, this dynamic will be maintained. After five years of hard work, the authors plan to collect qualitative and quantitative data from the students and supervisors to better assess the outcomes of these five years experience. This will allow us to adjust the several activities and determine new activities to help achieve the programme's goals.

The success of the Research Methodologies and Scientific Communication course in the Master on E-Business programme demonstrates the hard work and dedication of the institution's teachers, students and staff. We are proud of what we have achieved so far and are excited about the programme's future. With the proposed enhancements, we believe that we can provide an even better learning experience for our students and continue to produce graduates who are well-prepared for successful careers in the field of E-Business.

The journey of the Master on E-Business at the Business School of the Polytechnic of Porto is continuous, always striving for improvement and excellence.

References

Asaie, M., & Farsani, M. A. (2023). Surveying TEFL MA students' attitude towards research and research methodology course: A mixed research approach. Research in Post-Compulsory Education, 1–25. https://doi.org/10.1080/13596748.2023.2221120

Azevedo, A., Pinto, A., & Malta, M. (2019). On How to Build a Curriculum of an e-Business Master Course. Proceedings of the 16th International Joint Conference on E-Business and Telecommunications, 1, 222–230. https://doi.org/10.5220/0008120202220230

Daniel, B., Kumar, V., & Omar, N. (2018). Postgraduate conception of research methodology: Implications for learning and teaching. International Journal of Research & Method in Education, 41(2), 220–236. https://doi.org/10.1080/1743727X.2017.1283397

Gurung, R. A. R., & Stoa, R. (2020). A National Survey of Teaching and Learning Research Methods: Important Concepts and Faculty and Student Perspectives. Teaching of Psychology, 47(2), 111–120. https://doi.org/10.1177/0098628320901374

Authors' Biographies

Ana Azevedo is director of CEOS.PP research centre and Senior Lecturer at ISCAP, Polytechnic of Porto, Portugal. PhD in Information Systems and Technologies. Editor-in-chief of IJBIR; associate editor of IJTHI, IJDSST, and EJBRM; Advisory Board of IJILT. Regularly publishes in journals, conferences, and others. Research interest: Business Intelligence, E-Business, research methodologies.

Jose Azevedo is Senior Lecturer in the Mathematics Department, ISCAP, Polytechnic Institute of Porto, Portugal. He obtained is PhD in Education (Mathematics). Researcher at CEOS.PP. He published several articles in conferences and journals. His research interests are Analytics, Mathematics Education, E-Assessment, Financial Mathematics, Financial Time Series, Data Mining and E-Learning.

Mariana Curado Malta is Senior Lecturer at ISCAP, Polytechnic of Porto, Portugal. PhD in Technologies and Information Systems. Research interests: systematic ways of developing metadata application profiles (MAP). Author of the Me4MAP method. Works on several projects funded by Portuguese and European funds. Author of several scientific articles and book chapters.

Agostinho Sousa Pinto is Senior Lecturer at ISCAP, Polytechnic of Porto, Portugal. PhD in Information Systems and Technologies. Researcher at CEOS.PP and Algoritmi (University of Minho). He develops research on Organizational Knowledge Management, particularly on Shared Services. Developed a career as an IST Manager in large companies.

Accommodating Heterogeneity Challenges in Teaching Research Methodology: Evidence from an Indian Institution

Sreejith S S
Assistant Professor, School of Management Studies, National institute of Technology Calicut, Kerala, India
sreejithss@nitc.ac.in

Abstract: This case explains the pedagogical challenges faced due to the heterogeneity of students enrolled or a course in Research Methodology in an Indian Institution, and how an effective solution was identified. Research Methodology is a mandatory course to be completed by all the research scholars of this technology institution in India. There are research scholars from diverse area – science, engineering, technology, architecture, management, humanities and social sciences pursuing their PhD in the institute. Due to the student diversity and heterogeneity, it is challenging for the instructor to properly position the course in a manner so that all the students find it interesting as well able to relate to the philosophical underpinnings and specific methods used in their respective disciplines. After trying out different possibilities, the instructor designed a tool and an associated process based on heuristics which all the students can use to align their respective research designs. The tool was designed to have a 'T' design – which looks at the depth of the problem as well as accommodates multiple perspectives in their research design. The case details the development of the tool, the process and offers vignettes of handholding the students about the different stages of research progression: finding a researchable problem, developing a practical research objective, generating viable hypotheses, identifying, classifying and operationally defining the variables, and the research design phase. This template has gained popularity in the institute and more than 500 researchers are currently using this to develop a blue print for their research. This also serves the purpose of developing a skeletal research proposal. The delivery of the generic Research Methodology course has since been interesting, engaging and also creative.

Keywords: Heterogeneity, Research Methodology, Research Design Tool, Multi-disciplinary research, Creative Thinking

1. Background

The social, cultural, political, legal and technological environment that we live in, generate research problems regularly and challenge us on an everyday basis. While some of these can be solved using the available knowledge, a few of such problems require careful introspection and methodical approach so as to find a solution. A 'researchable' problem is hard to define and give shape to. While we may intuitively understand the existence of a problem, it often becomes a gargantuan task to articulate it and define it in a proper fashion. A single context can give raise to multiple problems. More precisely the same background information would trigger difference possibilities of manifestations of a problem. Just like the perception of individuals differ, so does their approach to problems. Some may look at the problem purely form an economical perspective, while other may look at through a technological lens, yet another could have a cultural angle to it and the fourth person may have an aesthetic viewpoint.

The multiple perspective of looking at a research problem should be encouraged, but can pose a challenge from a pedagogical aspect. While teaching research methods to a class of heterogeneous population of graduate students, one of the major challenges the instructor could face is how effectively can one demonstrate the concept of identifying a problem and slowly maturating it until the stage of research design. This is difficult because, the steps one chooses in the process would be highly dependent on the immediate previous step, which ultimately originates from the problem that has been identified.

From a pedagogical view point, the problem lied in this multi-perspective capability a potential research scenario has. For the earlier batches, an illustrative scenario will be provided; a possible problem will be identified and worked upon by the instructor, presuming that the students are able to understanding the technicalities of it. Usually the research design process follows these steps (Figure 1):

Figure 1: A research design process flow

Based on the theory they learn, they are expected to develop a research proposal. This will be a component for their examination where in the students will be evaluated based on the clarity and logical flow in developing a promising proposal.

Students often fail to understand the nuances in developing a compelling research proposal. There are a few mandatory inclusions in a standard research proposal. The strength of the proposal lies in how compelling ones research objective is and how pragmatic the research design are. This was the focus in teaching student to develop a research proposal. This was part of a compulsory course on Research Methodology for the students enrolled for a PhD programme in an Indian institution.

2. The Institution and Pedagogy

The institution in focus is primarily a technology institution which also has a focus on pure science, Architecture, Management, Economics and Language and Cultural Studies, besides engineering. There are several focus areas of engineering such as: Biotechnology, Computer Science, Civil Mechanical, Electrical, Electronics, Nano Science, and sciences: Mathematics, Physics and Chemistry, and Humanities, Social Science and Management. The students from all of these areas enroll for a common course in Research Methodology.

Initially the students are taught the theoretical concepts of research, as prescribed by standard text books. However the students were not able to think of the concepts from an application perspective. Their performances in exams were also not remarkable. This triggered to idea of familiarizing the students more from a practical aspect of how to pragmatically think and develop a logical research design.

The teaching process was redesigned to disseminate the same concepts, but which a special focus on the applicability of their creative thinking and designing. The modified pedagogy had three stages:

2.1 Stage 1: Learning the Theory and Paradigm of Research Methodology

The students enrolled in the course on Research Methodology are taught the principles of research from both philosophical as well as operational point of view. They are taught how to systematically navigate the research from a conceptual level to an operational level by identifying various elements in the research. This is spread across 15 lecture hours across three modules.

In Module 1, the scientific research philosophy is taught. The students are then taught about concepts, constructs, dimensions, indicators and variables. Basic ideas of logic – such as induction and deduction, relations, assumptions, conclusion and fallacies are also taught.

In Module 2 the students are taught how to develop research propositions and to propose testable hypotheses. Importantly, the students are hand held in designing an operational definition (and not dictionary definition) for the variables they have chosen, keeping in mind the measurability aspect.

Module 3: Further they are taught in detail about the research design, that includes: type of research (qualitative, quantitative, mixed and within each, an overview of the popular methods of research such as grounded theory, ethnography, or exploratory, causal, ex-post facto research or modeling research; sequential or concurrent design). It also includes the sampling design part (such as type of sampling – probabilistic or non-probabilistic - sampling unit, sample size, sample sufficiency). After this they are familiarized with the different data collection process such as qualitative (interviews, observation, group discussions) and qualitative (experimental, survey based or mathematical). Irrespective of their background, all students are taught the basic of experimental design (randomized control, Solomon four group design, Latin Square design). They are also taught about the measurement design (scales – nominal, ordinal, interval and ratio – instrument development, reliability and validity) and also the possible errors that could creep in.

Based on this, a template will be developed a shared with the students that has the following sections: Research Problem Identification, Research Objective; Hypothesis/ Model; Variable Identification; Operational Definition and Research design. The research design asks the students to explain the type of research; measurement design; sampling design, data collection plan and expected outcome. A sample template is shown in Figure 2.

After the students have understood the fundamental process of research, they are given a task that demands creative thinking (for problem generation) and logical reasoning for planning and designing the rest of the research. Due to their heterogeneity, a common problem background will be given. For example: A short paragraph about drones. This should enable them to think about drones form multiple perspectives. At this phase, the students would be encouraged to think in groups. If any student does not understand the background, then another common one would be identified and communicated.

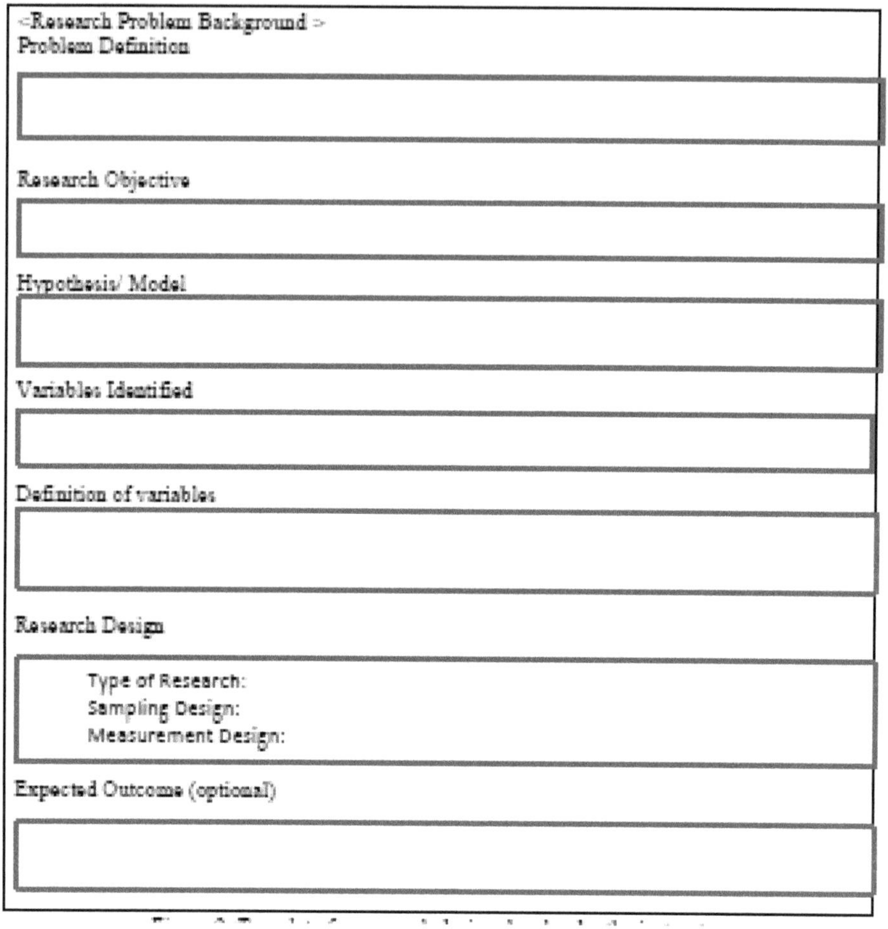

<Research Problem Background >

Problem Definition

Research Objective

Hypothesis/ Model

Variables Identified

Definition of variables

Research Design

Type of Research:
Sampling Design:
Measurement Design:

Expected Outcome (optional)

Figure 2: Template for research design develop by the instructor

2.2 Stage 2: Homogenous groups to identify possible research problems; choose one and develop a research design

After confirming that all the students understood the common research background, they are divided into smaller group of about 4-6 students. These small groups will be homogenous in nature, that is students from a common academic background will be put together (for example, students from Computer Science form a group, and students from Architecture form another group and so). They are expected to use the template to discuss further points and fill the template with one possible research perspective. They are given 15 minutes to identify a research problem and 40 minutes to develop the remaining details.

At the end of their assigned time, the students would submit the common research design to the instructor. Each student in the group will also have an individual copy for further discussion. Before evaluating the form, the instructor would distribute another set of the same blank template for Stage 3

2.3 Stage 3: Heterogeneous groups to discuss on possibilities of different research problems, and determine suitable research methods.

In this stage, the groups are reconstituted to make another set of small groups, with 406 members each. The groups are purposely deigned in a manner to include students from different academic backgrounds. Here the students discuss their previously identified problem,, and also listen to each other's' problem identified and possible research design. They also identify errors, suggest modifications and try to learn from each other, the different methods of solving a dimension of the same problem.

At stages 2 and 3 after the students complete their exercise, the instructor will give them feedback as a group. This will enable them, to appreciate the vastness of the problem. However once they have identified the problem, then the instructor would offer a detailed feedback, which enables them to depend their though process at a micro level. This 'T' model - model focusing on both the breadth and depth of a problem – enables the student to accommodate more diverse thoughts and also encourage them to focus deeper into how practical the research could be translated into action.

An illustration of the research design template with a few possible solutions is shown in Figures 3, 4 and 5, based on the following instruction and problem background.

1. Read the following problem background and generate a problem definition, identify and define variables (operational definition), propose hypotheses/model and design a research process.

Half of the largest cities in the world experience a scarcity of water. A mere 0.014% of all water on Earth is both fresh and easily accessible. Of the remaining water, 97% is saline and a little less than 3% is hard to access. Scientists, researchers, and governments are in continuous pursuit of desalinating water and making it accessible for all.

2.4 SOLUTION 1

Problem Definition

The distribution of desalinated water via water tankers is not cost effective and it takes longer to reach the households/ end users in the Western region of Chennai city.

Research Objective

To design an underground water supply mechanism using the shortest route for faster transportation of water to western region of Chennai city

Hypothesis/ Model

Heuristics and Simulation Model
Dijkstra's Algorithm
Log (Velocity of water) = Diameter+Density+Distance+Pressure+Error

Variables Identified

Velocity of Water; Diameter; Distance; Density; Pressure

Definition of variables

Velocity of Water = time taken by 1000 cc of water to cover a distance of 10 m through a HDPE pipe of diameter 15 cm
Diameter = diameter of the HDPE pipe (D1: 5 cm; D2: 10 cm; D3: 15 cm)
Distance = the minimum land distance (in km) from the desalination plants at Eastern Chennai (E1; E2 and E3) to the reservoir at Western Chennai (W1, W2, W3 and S4)
Density: Density of brine solution in the water before desalination (in ppm)
Pressure: Water pressure (Pa) for the entire distance for a level layout of pipes

Research Design

Type of Research: Modelling and Simulation (Mathematical Modeling; genetic Algorithm and Software based simulation]
Measurement Design: Interval and Ratio scale
Sampling Design: Random sampling for simulation
Data Source: Secondary data

Figure 3: Illustration 1 of a possible research design development

Data Source: Secondary data

2.5 SOLUTION 2

Problem Definition

Children who consume desalinated water on a regular basis suffer from increased pancreatic diseases.

Research Objective

To test the effect of adding pancreatic enzymes in desalinated water to reduce the frequency of occurrence of pancreatic diseases in children

Hypothesis/ Model

Hypothesis
H1: Adding 0.03 ppm of pancreatic enzyme to desalinated water before distribution significantly reduces the frequency of occurrence of pancreatic diseases in children.

Variables Identified

Pancreatic diseases; Children

Definition of variables

Pancreatic diseases: Persistence presence of diseases such as pancreatitis; vomiting; diarrhea for more than 3 days
Children: Humans less than 12 years of age

Research Design

Type of Research: Experimental Research (Field Experiment)
Measurement Design: Questionnaire (with rating scale)
Sampling Design: Stratified random sampling (from three locations of the city)
Data Source: Primary

Figure 4: Illustration 2 of a possible research design development

2.6 SOLUTION 3

Problem Definition

Toxic brine due to desalination adversely affects the coastal and marine ecosystem in the coastal regions of India

Research Objective

To explore and identify the magnitude of impact caused by copper chloride in brine due to desalination in the lifespan of **Portunus sanguinolentus** (**a sea crab**) in the southern coast of Karnataka

Hypothesis/ Model

Hypothesis
H1: Copper chloride present in pre-treatment process of brine decreases the level of oxygen required for sustaining the life of Portunus sanguinolentus (a species of crab).

Variables Identified

Toxic Brine, Copper Chloride concentration, Oxygen Level, Lifespan of Portunus sanguinolentus

Definition of variables

Toxic Brine: Presence of copper chloride greater than 0.05 mg per liter
Copper Chloride Concentration: The proportion of $CuCl_2$ in one litre of sea water near the desalination plant
Oxygen Level: Level of oxygen in mg per litre of sea water
Lifespan of crabs: Life of Portunus sanguinolentus live in years

Research Design

Type of Research: Experimentation and Observation
Measurement Design: Ratio scale
Sampling Design: Random sampling
Data Source: Primary data

Figure 5: Illustration 3 of a possible research design development

These are only three of the many possible solutions. Depending on one's cognitive orientation and academic background, the student can identify multiple problems form the same problem background. Based on these the students are expected to develop a research proposal.

3. Student feedback

The students were apprehensive at the beginning, suggesting that the theoretical fundamentals served their purpose of writing a proposal. But they were nudged to participate, and sometimes even threatened by reminding them that it is a mandatory component for evaluation. After the initial group formation and instructions, when the objective was conveyed, students actively participated in the discussions. Students said that the exercise was engaging, and making them think which otherwise they would not have. They also liked the idea of listening to multiple perspectives of the same problem background from others. Overall, it is quite a change from the long theory classes and the class was active.

4. Evaluation

A statistical analysis was conducted on the marks scored by the students for research proposal before and after teaching them how to develop the proposal using the template. The score was graded on a 10 point scale (10 being the highest possible score). The mean scores obtained (before 7.27/10 and after 8.41/10) was statistically significant (t value = 5.64, df = 257, $p<0.001$). There were no control variables though.

5. Conclusion

The paper elaborates a template that is used to teach the nuances of research design to a group of heterogeneous group of students. The template was developed and deployed as a part of course on Research Methodology, which students belonging to different academic background enroll for. Due to this heterogeneity it is challenging to teach them the intricacies and peculiarities of research design. The proposed template for research design, encourages the student to think deep in their chosen method and also think broad by listening to the viewpoints of other researchers. The template use a generic scenario from which the researcher need to develop one possible research problem, and come up with an objective. They should conduct literature review and develop a conceptual framework based on that. Variables are identified, classified and operationally defined. Hypotheses are generated. Research design including the type of research, sampling process, data collection and measurement plan are to be chosen. The template has evidently helped the students think better focusing on how well can this be used to translate their research problems into action and also to develop good quality research proposals. A major limitation in this template is the lack of literature review. Hypotheses were generated based on the assumption that there's enough theoretical support to their objectives and propositions. To build a strong hypothesis, and proceed with the research design, a framework based on theoretical and conceptual knowledge needs to be developed and articulated.

6. Future Plans

The template can be extended to include Literature Review as well. A synthesis matrix can be a part of the template along with building a conceptual or theoretical framework to establish the significance of the current research. The template can be subject to a wider reliability check and can be standardized in the future to serve as a basis for enhancing their writing skills.

Author Biography

Sreejith S S is an Assistant Professor with the School of Management Studies, National Institute of Technology Calicut, Kerala, India. Sreejith S S has a PhD from the Indian Institute of Science in the area of Human Resource Management. His research interest is majorly in Behavioral Science. He has published in the areas of Employee Performance Management, Rewards and Recognition, Performance Evaluation and HR Analytics. He teaches Behavioral Science and Human Resource Management to MBA students and Research Methodology to PhD students.

"Is this Clear to you?": Statistical Reasoning and Coding in Teaching Quantitative Methods

Dr Igor Tkalec

Assistant Professor of Social Data Science, Social Data Institute, University College London, UK

i.tkalec@ucl.ac.uk

Abstract: Programming/coding has become an integral part of teaching quantitative social science at universities. It has been observed that coding has been over-emphasised in quantitative social sciences courses arguably at the expense of statistical reasoning. The "Is this clear to you?" teaching initiative aims to reassert vital importance of statistical reasoning and highlight that the role of coding within social sciences is instrumental. The initiative entails incremental changes concerning class organisation and class delivery .

1. Introduction and context

Quantitative methods and statistics courses consist of lectures and lab/practical sessions. Lectures prevalently discuss conceptual fundamentals and thus directly address statistical reasoning. Statistical reasoning is defined as making sense and interpreting statistical information that is underpinned by the understanding of statistical ideas and concepts (Garfield 2002). Lab/practical sessions then apply conceptual knowledge in a programming language (e.g., R, Python, Stata, Matlab).

Programming/coding has become an integral element of social science degree programmes due to its high demand on the labour market. Nonetheless, over-emphasis on coding in statistics classes arguably comes at a price. In-class observations and fruitful exchange with colleagues who teach quantitative social science indicate the following: coding has overshadowed reasoning in class delivery. In other words, students care more about their code showing no errors than about understanding why they started to code in the first place (i.e., to analyse a problem and provide data-informed solution to it) and about making sense of the code output (i.e., interpreting numbers, relations, coefficients, visuals in the context of a given problem through statistical reasoning).

Social science undergraduate students with little or no prior experience with statistics, data science or quantitative methods in general tend to get overwhelmed by coding. This arguably induces a well-known phenomenon of statistics anxiety among university students. Statistics anxiety is defined as situation-specific negative emotional reaction to engagement with statistics in any form (e.g., data collection, interpretation of statistical analyses) (Bradstreet 1996; Onwuegbuzie 2000; 2004; Koh and Zawi 2014). The roots of statistics anxiety include bad experience in learning mathematics in primary and secondary education, attitudes towards statistics and ability to learn statistics (this process can be compared to learning a second language) (Lalonde and Gardner 1993). The anxiety demonstrates itself through perception of usefulness of statistics (students who perceive statistics as irrelevant tend to be more anxious), fear of statistical language (e.g., formulas, symbols, notations), fear of application of statistical knowledge (e.g., comprehension of quantitative academic article) and interpersonal anxiety (reluctance to ask for help from peers or lecturers) (Onwuegbuzie 1997). Statistics anxiety has far-reaching negative effects on students' wellbeing that may entail depression, frustration, non-optimal learning environment, panic, and mental anguish (Onwuegbuzie 2004). For instance, the anxiety "pushes" students in statistics (and mathematics) classes to memorise the procedures rather than understand them (Schacht and Stewart 1990). In addition, statistics anxiety may lead to avoidance of quantitative courses whatsoever and, consequently, professional careers that entail quantitative component (Wilson 1997).

Studies have recognised that changes in class organisation, adaptation of teaching style and adjustments in class contents can help mitigate the effects of statistics anxiety (see e.g., Forte 1995; Schacht and Stewart 1990; Smith 1998; Paxton 2006; Decesare 2007). To illustrate, in order to motivate sociology students, Paxton (2006: 68) gives "students a list of common first occupations for people with a BA in sociology, their starting salaries, and whether the occupation uses statistics or not". In addition, Ziv (1988) found that the lecturer's usage of jokes or cartoons in teaching statistics had a positive effect on overall performance on the final exam (see Schacht and Stewart 1990). Moreover, cooperative learning, small group tutorials and practice of speaking statistics in class environment also showed as pertinent in decreasing statistics anxiety (Forte 1995).

Against this backdrop and in order to mitigate or even prevent the above situation, teaching initiative under the "Is this clear to you?" moto reasserts fundamental importance of statistical reasoning in teaching of social science statistics and quantitative methods especially in relation to coding. In other words, the initiative emphasises that the role of coding in social sciences setting ought to be instrumental. This suggests that coding represents the means (the instrument) for achieving the goal that is to answer a quantitative social science question/problem. Yet, such answers cannot be developed or interpreted without statistical reasoning skills. To this end, statistical reasoning enables knowledge extraction from data, which is the ultimate goal of quantitative data analyses.

It is vital to highlight that the initiative does not aim to undermine the importance of coding and coding skills in any way. Due to its utility and applicability in various analytical and problem-solving contexts, coding is and should remain necessary element of quantitative courses in social science degree programs.

Specific objectives of the initiative include:

- To re-emphasise the importance of statistical reasoning and portray coding as instrumental in quantitative social science courses through didactical changes concerning class organisation.
- To make explicit references to the crucial role of statistical reasoning in solving quantitative social science problems through modified teaching style and in-class student exercises.

The initiative has been observed, developed and implemented within one undergraduate course *Introduction to Econometrics* at Sciences Po Paris; one walk-in weekly support session – *Coding Therapy* at University College London; and one graduate seminar on *Quantitative Research Design* at Centre International Formation Europennee and LUISSS School of Government (Rome and Nice). Inclusion of multiple universities is an advantage as the initiative can be observed and implemented across different academic degree programs, student backgrounds and academic cultures. The initiative is still ongoing.

2. The infrastructure: implementation of the initiative

Thus far, the initiative has been implemented through multiple incremental changes concerning both class organisation and class delivery. Concerning the former, four manoeuvres have been implemented. First, a pre-course survey was developed in order to determine the level of students' familiarity with fundamental statistical concepts and experience with programming skills. More specifically, the survey included questions such as: *have you ever taken an introductory statistics/quantitative methods course at university level*; *could you define and distinguish between interval and ratio variable*; *could you interpret alpha significance level and p-value*; *have you ever used software for statistical analysis (e.g., R, Stata, SPSS, Python, etc.)* to name a few. The results of the pre-course survey indicated that the majority of students are not familiar with fundamental statistical concepts nor a programming language. These observations were of great help in preparing course materials and defining learning objectives. For example, the class then started with the discussion of the research process in general including concepts such as data observation and indictors instead of directly going into fundamental statistical concepts such as variance and correlation.

Second, the so-called 'conversation lecture' was introduced. The lecture occurs in week one of the course(s) and invites students to reflect on methodology courses in general and the importance of statistical reasoning. More specifically, the lecture contextualises relevance and application of statistics across different sectors of the labour market and discusses the general role of numbers and statistics in society (e.g., (mis)usage of statistics for marketing or political purposes). In addition, the lecture gives particular attention to the above-defined phenomenon of statistics anxiety. Students are asked to talk about their eventual anxiety toward numbers, mathematics and statistics. Sources of such anxiety are then discussed (e.g., bad experience in a previous course; poor grade in mathematics during secondary education). Existence of such anxiety is then normalised. In this context, the essential point the lecture aims to convey is that the current course setting accepts eventual anxiety and appropriately addresses it notably through students' input and feedback. For example, if students feel more comfortable and productive to do the take-home assignments in pairs rather than individually, the course accommodates for this. Such an inclusive approach has been impactful especially in terms of students' creativity and quality of project-based assignments. The conversation lecture yielded positive results – students appear more relaxed during the semester, active course participation rate has increased and overall student performance has slightly improved.

Third, course sessions that entail coding are introduced only half-way through the course during the semester (from week six onward). Coding in introductory statistics course is arguably an overwhelming experience for students with no prior experience. The aim of this manoeuvre has thus been to prevent or at least mitigate such student impressions. To this end, the first six weeks of the course have been only conceptual and exclusively emphasise statistical reasoning. Then, in the last six weeks of the course, the conceptual discussions have been directly implemented into a programming environment. To illustrate, in week two (as the conversation lecture occupied week one) basic statistical concepts such as variable types, mean, median and standard deviation were discussed conceptually. In week six (the first week of coding), the same concepts were implemented in the programming environment. This pattern applies to other conceptual topics such as correlation, bivariate linear regression, multivariate linear regression, regression diagnostics, and data visualisation. Hence, each conceptual session has its programming counterpart.

Such organisation of the course has highlighted multiple benefits. First, it has enabled repetitive encounter with fundamental concepts and subjects. Second, before embarking on their coding journey, students were conceptually familiar with the concepts they were expected to implement in a programming language. Third, decreased amount of coding session emphasised coding's (secondary) instrumental role in relation to statistical reasoning. Although students spent less time engaging with programming environment, fewer coding session were still sufficient to provide a fundamental overview of the programming language. Social science courses seldom offer advanced level of coding skills as coding learning curve is arguably steep and individual (see Crestani and Sperber 2010; Saito and Yamaura 2013). Instead, (introductory) courses primarily provide extensive familiarity with a programming environment (e.g., navigating through window panes of a code editor; getting and installing packages for particular type of analysis, pointing to resources for help and debugging, etc.).

Fourth, revision and feedback sessions were introduced. One course session (after half of the course content have been covered and immediately prior the deadline for the mid-term assignment) has been dedicated to comprehensive revision. Students are incentivised (with an extra point on their mid-term assignment) to lead the revision session by demonstrating statistical reasoning. A volunteer student would come out and sketch and explain the thus far discussed concepts on a white board. During the student's elaboration, the lecturer notes eventual omitted content and/or mistakes. After the elaboration, other students are invited to add, re-clarify and/or re-emphasise some of the covered concepts/topics. Moreover, most of the last week's session was dedicated to feedback. Here ideas on project-focused final assignments are discussed. Students are encouraged to give peer-to-peer constructive feedback. The lecturer also provides extensive feedback on the assignment ideas (e.g., on credibility of secondary data sources). It is important to highlight that revision and feedback sessions have increased student ownership of the course, which often turns into better overall performance. These sessions additionally emphasise that the course has been devised to the students' benefit.

In addition to class organisation manoeuvres, the initiative has been implemented through three changes in class delivery. First, a whiteboard has been preferred over power point. Power point presentations have been contested in terms of their effectiveness in higher education (see Craig and Amernic 2006; Baker et al. 2018). Using whiteboard during conceptual sessions in teaching statistics has advantages. To start with, drawing on a whiteboard underpins constant dynamic during the class. Additionally, as statistical analyses are often organised in sequential steps, the initiative has shown that it is easier for students to follow the transition between the steps on the whiteboard. To illustrate, a simple hypothesis test can be organised in sequential steps starting from forming hypotheses from theory, then defining the relevant concepts, then selecting indicators and variables, then collecting the data and finally conducting the test. Moreover, the usage of whiteboard, at least to some extent (as the coding session require the usage of computers), balances out students' over-exposure to electronics on day-to-day basis that is potentially harmful to their wellbeing (see e.g., Caumo et al. 2020). Furthermore, it has been noticed that the usage of whiteboard coincides with students opting to take class notes by hand rather than on an electronic device such as laptop or tablet.

Second, the relationship (or a tension) between statistical reasoning and coding during classes have been continuously, repetitively, and explicitly referred to during the classes. Here the point is for students to understand that reasoning is a necessary pre-condition for coding (i.e., you ought to know what to ask a programming language to do) and, vitally, analytical problem-solving. In other words, the role of coding in a social science context is instrumental meaning that it is a means to implement the reasoning (as reasoning may be implemented in an environment that does not require any code). Here examples from students' potential future employment environment are often used. For example, it is emphasised that their managers would not be interested in the code itself, but in the reasoning– a data-driven solution to a given problem (e.g., should we as a company open another branch?).

Third, in-class 'code interpretation' exercise (as complementary to code writing) that nurtures statistical reasoning was developed. Students are given a take-away coding exercise. In the subsequent coding session, students are invited (and incentivised by an extra point for their final assignment) to conduct the exercise by explaining code snippets and, crucially, linking them to statistical reasoning. A volunteer student does the exercise. They are expected to divide the code in separate elements (e.g., programming data object, functions, argument of a function) and discuss their purpose in respect to the given task/problem (i.e., statistical reasoning). Additionally, the emphasis is on the interpretation of the code output, which is the essence of statistical reasoning within a quantitative social science course. Other students are invited to help the volunteer student in case they run into obstacles.

3. The challenges

Three prominent challenges occurred in development of the manoeuvres and their implementation. First, concerning development, as the issue the initiative tackles is yet to be explored, manoeuvres lacked concrete scientific grounding. In other words, there was a lack of (social science) studies to serve as benchmarks to shape the manoeuvres and expectations behind them. Nevertheless, widely developed statistics anxiety literature served as a contextual guide. Moreover, my extensive previous experience as a learner/student of statistics and coding served as a reference in developing the manoeuvres.

Second, regarding implementation, it has been challenging to balance implicit/latent and explicit/manifest styles of manoeuvre implementation. Had all of them been implemented explicitly, this may have turned out overwhelming and counter-productive for students. Therefore, manoeuvres concerning pre-course survey, introduction of coding session only in the second half of the course and usage of whiteboard have been implemented implicitly ('under the radar') – meaning that they did not include an explicit link to the relationship between statistical reasoning and coding (yet they still contributed to addressing the issue). The aim was for students to perceive these manoeuvres as given rather than as direct responses to the potential tension between statistical reasoning and coding.

Third, it has been challenging to get students to understand that coding is not 'bad' or unnecessary and that it should not be dismissed whatsoever (if there are alternatives). To avoid such a negative (and ultimately wrong) perceptions of coding, I have been elaborating on its important, yet instrumental role (in a data project environment) in respect to statistical reasoning and answering social science research questions. To this end, as explicitly mentioned in the introduction, this initiative does not aim to undermine the importance of coding and coding skills (for social sciences and beyond) in any way.

4. Students' reception of the initiative

Students have been, contrary to the initial expectations, generally rather receptive and embracing of the initiative. This has been confirmed during the last sessions of the courses as well as during feedback sessions. In addition, official students' evaluations as well indicate that the manoeuvres have been accepted by students. Moreover, positive feedback via individual emails from students in which they actually refer to importance of statistical reasoning was received.

The initial expectations were not so optimistic. The strongest scepticism was that the initiative's manoeuvres may put off students with somewhat 'abstract' or not as exciting idea and practice of statistical reasoning (at least in relation to coding which is a very concrete exercise). This scepticism was grounded in current trends on the labour market that is in high demand for coding skills across almost all industries. To get a better grasp of the labour market, random job listings for data/business analysts and policy officers were briefly analysed. The listings indeed required some coding experience, yet they tend not to mention statistical reasoning (which they actually expect to see from their future employees) in any way. Hence, the expectation was that students would not be so embracing to put extra emphasis on statistical reasoning and treat coding as instrumental. Luckily, this has not been the case.

5. The learning outcomes

Arguably, the overarching achievement of the initiative is that it has recognised that the potential tension between statistical reasoning and coding in quantitative social science is indeed an issue. As the initiative was implemented through incremental manoeuvres regrading class organisation and class delivery, it does not entail quantifiable outcomes *per se*. The only quantifiable measure to be mentioned is an increase in overall student performance. Yet, without a proper experimental design, it is uncertain to what extent the manoeuvres were direct causes of it (an expectation would be that the implemented manoeuvres had a significant and direct impact of the overall student performance). Hence, in a medium-term, the effect of the manoeuvres is planned to first be measured and then quantitatively analysed.

Nevertheless, the initiative yielded observable qualitative changes/outcomes. First, within the initiative, a change in overall students' focus has been observed. An indication of this is that their discussion questions have become problem- rather than code-oriented. For example, while discussing ideas for the final data analysis project assignment, students asked whether a certain selection of variables made sense for a given research problem instead of, for instance, focusing on how to execute a model within coding environment (these kind of questions were rather common before the implementation of the initiative's manoeuvres). Along the same lines, students have started inquiring about problem-oriented issues in their potential future employment.

Second, students have become more relaxed (or less anxious) in regard to research methodology courses and statistics in particular. More precisely, the impression is that they have become more embracing of it. This is a vital observation as, at least in my thus far experience, methodology and statistics courses are not among the students' favourites. To this end, students expressed extra interest in the subject matter, for example, by inquiring about credible online learning sources.

Third, as a likely consequence of the above two, students have become more confident in their knowledge, which in turn resulted in significant boost in in-class active participation. For example, during the first two classes, roughly 15 percent of students actively participated during classes. This has increased roughly to 60 percent by the end of the semester. As a response to increased active participation, by the end of the semester, preparation of lectures had to account for an increased time of direct student input.

6. Plans to further develop the initiative

The next stage of development of the initiative entails two parts. First, in collaboration with colleagues who teach quantitative social science, we have contemplated how to directly include students into the discussion. The aim is to set up a student-inclusive channel such as a periodic or annual student consultation event in order to further improve the overall teaching quality and class delivery mechanisms in respect to the relationship between statistical reasoning and coding. The student consultation is planned to be organised through cohort-targeted focus groups, from which course-specific as well as department-level guidance on how to enhance the role of statistical reasoning in quantitative social science courses could be developed (and then, of course, implemented).

Second, organisation and delivery of extra (support) sessions that exclusively focus on statistical reasoning will be considered. This step ought to be preceded by consolidation of lecturers' in-class observations across courses as well as across cohorts (from first to third year undergraduate). The extra sessions undertake a holistic approach to fundamentals of statistics so that their content is applicable across a range of courses. Thus, fundamental concepts are discussed in respect to their purpose in addressing a quantitative problem. For instance, why does one need to look at frequency distributions; what is the purpose of measures of central tendency; why prediction in social sciences tends to be imperfect; why does one work with samples rather than populations in quantitative research, to name a few.

In general, the next stages of development of the initiative should not omit the role artificial intelligence (AI) and its accompanying tools such as ChatGPT as they have become an omnipresent topic for universities especially in the context of academic misconduct, plagiarism and assessment. This is especially pertinent for quantitative courses that include coding, as AI tools are able to effectively produce code in various programming languages in a blink of an eye. To this end, it is arguably counter-productive (or impossible?) to completely prohibit students to use AI tools during their studies and engagement with statistics. Instead, efforts to embrace such tools and exploit their advantages appear prudent. In the context of the presented initiative, usage of AI tools potentially opens more space to reinstate the vital importance of statistical reasoning.

References

Baker, James P., Alan K. Goodboy, Nicholas D. Bowman, and Alyssa A. Wright. 2018. 'Does Teaching with PowerPoint Increase Students' Learning? A Meta-Analysis'. *Computers & Education* 126 (November): 376–87. https://doi.org/10.1016/j.compedu.2018.08.003.

Bradstreet, Thomas E. 1996. 'Teaching Introductory Statistics Courses so That Nonstatisticians Experience Statistical Reasoning'. *The American Statistician* 50 (1): 69–78.

Caumo, Guilherme Hidalgo, Daniel Spritzer, Alicia Carissimi, and André Comiran Tonon. 2020. 'Exposure to Electronic Devices and Sleep Quality in Adolescents: A Matter of Type, Duration, and Timing'. *Sleep Health* 6 (2): 172–78. https://doi.org/10.1016/j.sleh.2019.12.004.

Craig, Russell J., and Joel H. Amernic. 2006. 'PowerPoint Presentation Technology and the Dynamics of Teaching'. *Innovative Higher Education* 31 (3): 147–60. https://doi.org/10.1007/s10755-006-9017-5.

Crestani, Marcus, and Michael Sperber. 2010. 'Experience Report: Growing Programming Languages for Beginning Students'. *ACM SIGPLAN Notices* 45 (9): 229–34. https://doi.org/10.1145/1932681.1863576.

Decesare, Michael. 2007. '"Statistics Anxiety" Among Sociology Majors: A First Diagnosis and Some Treatment Options'. *Teaching Sociology* 35 (4): 360–67. https://doi.org/10.1177/0092055X0703500405.

Forte, James A. 1995. 'Teaching Statistics without Sadistics'. *Journal of Social Work Education* 31 (2): 204–18. https://doi.org/10.1080/10437797.1995.10672258.

Garfield, Joan. 2002. 'The Challenge of Developing Statistical Reasoning'. *Journal of Statistics Education* 10 (3): 2. https://doi.org/10.1080/10691898.2002.11910676.

Koh, Denise, and Mohd Khairi Zawi. 2014. 'Statistics Anxiety among Postgraduate Students'. *International Education Studies* 7 (13): 166–74. https://doi.org/10.5539/ies.v7n13p166.

Lalonde, Richard N., and Robert C. Gardner. 1993. 'Statistics as a Second Language? A Model for Predicting Performance in Psychology Students.' *Canadian Journal of Behavioural Science / Revue Canadienne Des Sciences Du Comportement* 25 (1): 108–25. https://doi.org/10.1037/h0078792.

Onwuegbuzie, Anthony J. 1997. 'Writing a Research Proposal: The Role of Library Anxiety, Statistics Anxiety, and Composition Anxiety'. *Library & Information Science Research* 19 (1): 5–33. https://doi.org/10.1016/S0740-8188(97)90003-7.

———. 2000. 'Statistics Anxiety and the Role of Self-Perceptions'. *The Journal of Educational Research* 93 (5): 323–30. https://doi.org/10.1080/00220670009598724.

———. 2004. 'Academic Procrastination and Statistics Anxiety'. *Assessment & Evaluation in Higher Education* 29 (1): 3–19. https://doi.org/10.1080/0260293042000160384.

Paxton, Pamela. 2006. 'Dollars and Sense: Convincing Students That They Can Learn and Want to Learn Statistics'. *Teaching Sociology* 34 (1): 65–70. https://doi.org/10.1177/0092055X0603400106.

Saito, Daisuke, and Tsuneo Yamaura. 2013. 'A New Approach to Programming Language Education for Beginners with Top-down Learning'. In *Proceedings of 2013 IEEE International Conference on Teaching, Assessment and Learning for Engineering (TALE)*, 752–55. https://doi.org/10.1109/TALE.2013.6654538.

Schacht, Steven, and Brad J. Stewart. 1990. 'What's Funny about Statistics? A Technique for Reducing Student Anxiety'. *Teaching Sociology* 18 (1): 52. https://doi.org/10.2307/1318231.

Smith, Gary. 1998. 'Learning Statistics by Doing Statistics'. *Journal of Statistics Education* 6 (3): 5. https://doi.org/10.1080/10691898.1998.11910623.

Wilson, Vicki. 1997. 'Factors Related to Anxiety in the Graduate Statistics Classroom'. In . Memphis.

Author's Biography

Igor Tkalec is lecturer in social data science at Social Data Institute, University College London interested in social policy and applied data science. Prior to joining UCL, Igor was a research fellow at the European University Institute. He obtained his PhD at the University of Luxembourg.

www.ingramcontent.com/pod-product-compliance
Ingram Content Group UK Ltd.
Pitfield, Milton Keynes, MK11 3LW, UK
UKHW020234250726
13967UKWH00001B/369

9 781914 587788